Race and Ethnic Relations
in the First Person

RACE AND ETHNIC RELATIONS IN THE FIRST PERSON

Alfred T. Kisubi and
Michael A. Burayidi

Westport, Connecticut
London

Library of Congress Cataloging-in-Publication Data

Kisubi, Alfred.
   Race and ethnic relations in the first person / Alfred T. Kisubi
and Michael A. Burayidi.
     p.   cm.
   Includes bibliographical references (p.) and index.
   ISBN 0–275–96069–2 (alk. paper)
   1. United States—Race relations—Case studies. 2. United States—
Ethnic relations—Case studies. 3. College students—United
States—Interviews. I. Burayidi, Michael A. II. Title.
E185.615.K565   1998
305.8′00973—dc21   97–26903

British Library Cataloguing in Publication Data is available.

Library of Congress Catalog Card Number: 97–26903
ISBN: 0–275–96069–2

First published in 1998

Praeger Publishers, 88 Post Road West, Westport, CT 06881
An imprint of Greenwood Publishing Group, Inc.

Printed in the United States of America

The paper used in this book complies with the
Permanent Paper Standard issued by the National
Information Standards Organization (Z39.48–1984).

10 9 8 7 6 5 4 3 2 1

To the memory of Dr. Martin Luther King, Jr.,
Whose legacy of *agape* shall never die,
But incessantly shall provide a basis
For continued efforts to overcome domination.

And to President Nelson Mandela,
Whose agony and triumphant rise
Became a beacon of tolerance for us,
And all the Universe to see.

To these and others, who envision
A community of humans, in which all are free.

Contents

Preface

The verdict in the O. J. Simpson criminal case brought to the fore the deep racial divide that still plagues America. The trial of the century tested the very fabric of American society. Controversial issues regarding sex, race, White wife and Black husband, White police and Black suspect, fame, justice, and fairness all surfaced in the trial. The case rekindled the perennial race problem that has haunted the United States since the country's foundation. Whites were shocked and angry at the verdict while Blacks rejoiced that one of their members had escaped what they regarded as the unfair judicial system in the country.

This different reaction of the two races to the verdict baffles outside observers: How is it that a wealthy country like the United States, which can send someone to the moon and back to earth, is unable to solve its racial problems? How is it possible for people who reside in the same country to have such differing views about the justice system? How does one explain the different reactions to the verdict by Blacks and Whites? *Race and Ethnic Relations in the First Person* addresses these questions through the stories of individuals from different socioeconomic, racial, and ethnic backgrounds. Through their stories, we are able to discern why the reactions of Blacks and Whites to the O. J. Simpson verdict were so different. The stories also provide us with clues for addressing the fears and obstacles that keep the various races and ethnic groups apart.

Race relations has, since at least the 1920s, been studied by sociologists such as Robert Park, Everett Hughes, and Louis Wirth. *Race and Ethnic Relations in the First Person* contributes to this body of knowledge through the candid personal accounts of the life stories of people from diverse socioeconomic and cultural backgrounds. By so doing, the book demonstrates the impact that the socializing agents of family, educational institutions, and the workplace have on the worldview of people.

We hope that this short selection of personal accounts about racial/ethnic relations will make some contribution to political, policy, economic, educational, and home discussions in the United States and perhaps elsewhere. If there is any message implied in this book, we hope it is a reaffirmation of the need to recognize the fundamental unity and equality of all human beings regardless of color, race, religion, or gender.

Acknowledgments

We acknowledge our African upbringing, especially the efforts exerted by our families, communities, and educational institutions in Uganda and Ghana to ensure that we became lifetime students of the human condition.

We would like to thank the following people who directly or indirectly helped us during the decade of this study: Charles J. Carleson, Landon Kirchner, Caroline Kadel, Chuck Bishop, Barbara and Matt Campbell, Dick and Elly Dawson, Fred Krebs, Leon Berger, Robert L. Perry, Tom and Sarah Crane, Dr. Fred Whitehead, Verle Muhrer, Carl Bettis, Sharon Eiker, and Dr. Jeff Longhoffer. We are also grateful to Drs. Janet Hagen, Ann Frisch, Karen Muench, Shirley Wilbert, and Henry Winterfelt, who encouraged our philosophical, sociological, and poetic global outlook.

We would like to thank the late Dr. Hugh W. Speer and Dr. Marie Peck, who got us involved in the reconstruction of incidents that led to the landmark civil rights cases in Kansas, such as the *Webb et al. v. School District 90* (South Park School, Merriam, Kansas), *Brown v. Board of Education of Topeka* (Brown I), Brown II, and Brown III. These cases continue to play an important role in American education.

The Martin Luther King, Jr. exhibit that we assisted Dr. Speer in setting up helped us to learn more about African American and minority issues in education. Also, the discussions we held with Linda Brown Smith and Cheryl Brown Henderson (plaintiff in Brown III, 1985–86; daughters of Oliver Brown, plaintiff in *Brown v. Board of Education*, 1951) made us aware of the racial tensions in the United States. We are grateful for this encounter.

The panel discussion by Ed Beasley, Dan Levine, and William M. Tuttle, "Before and after Brown: History and Impact of Brown, I, II, III," impacted us greatly and helped shape the questions that later became the center of our quest to understand racial relations in the Midwest and beyond, and their impact on the socialization of the young. We are grateful to our families and friends for their support and patience while this project was underway. We would also like to thank Mary Bleser for proofreading the manuscript and offering useful suggestions for clarifying our writing and for formatting the book. Above all, we are profoundly indebted to the hundreds of students who so willingly participated in this study and shared their experiences with us, and hopefully the general public at large.

Race and Ethnic Relations in the First Person

1

Introduction

In 1903 W. E. B. Du Bois wrote that the problem of the twentieth century is the problem of the color line. On the eve of the twenty-first century, the color line might seem a little blurred but nonetheless very much drawn. There are no longer separate White and Black fountains and restrooms, and there is more interracial mingling now than in Du Bois's time. Despite this progress, Blacks and Whites are still very much estranged. The O. J. Simpson verdict graphically showed that American society is deeply divided by race. When the first words of "not guilty" were heard from the clerk in the O. J. Simpson trial, there were either cheers or jeers. African Americans jumped for joy while Whites were angry with disbelief. This trial of the century, with all its taboos—sex, race, White woman/Black man, White police/Black suspect, and others—was a trial of America itself. To some people, the dream of brotherhood seems even more distant now than when Martin Luther King, Jr. spoke from the steps of the Lincoln Memorial in 1963. "I have a dream," King said. "I have a dream that one day, on the red hills of Georgia, the sons of former slaves and the sons of former slave owners will be able to sit together at the table of brotherhood."

Yet today, the opinions that the races hold of each other are diametrically opposite. In a survey carried out by James Patterson and Peter Kim on 1990 stereotypes, 61% of Whites agreed that African Americans were athletic, 33% said African Americans were criminal, 31% agreed that African Americans were violent, and 29% said they were lazy. On the other hand, 49% of African American respondents said that Whites were racists, 21% said Whites were greedy, and 14% said that Whites were dangerous (Patterson and Kim 1991, 183).

Patterson and Kim revealed in their interviews that Whites put the blame on Blacks for not taking advantage of the opportunities America offers. To three-fourths of White people interviewed, the recent success of Asian Americans confirms their low opinion about Blacks. But the Black respondents felt that the old ascriptive system that favors Whites over minority groups still remains in place and that African Americans lack the opportunities that are available to Whites.

This difference in the opinions and attitudes of one race toward the other has been the subject of research for decades. Several papers and books have been published that seek to explain how people come to form opinions about races and ethnic groups that are different from their own. Although there is no generally accepted theory to explain the development of racist behavior and attitudes, some of the theories so far advanced include the "personality needs" theory, the competition theory, the exploitation theory, the caste theory, the scapegoating theory, the structural theory, and the socialization theory (Schaefer 1990). These theories have been well documented in the literature and do not need extensive discussion here. For the most part, however, the theories discuss race relations at the aggregate and generic level and the individual and microcircumstances that help to shape individual attitudes are lost in the theoretical discussions. This book provides a microlevel account of the socialization of people, and the nature in which family, peer groups, school, religious groups, and the workplace shape people's perceptions of racial and ethnic groups who are different from theirs. It, therefore, differs from previous work in this area because it is a first person account of the interacting socioeconomic forces that influence people's perceptions of other races and ethnic groups.

RESEARCH PROCEDURE

This book is based on a ten-year study of college students in three Midwestern states. Some three hundred sociology, human services, and education students in four colleges were asked to write reflective essays on how family, schools, religious groups, and the workplace have had an effect in shaping their perceptions and attitudes of different racial and ethnic groups. In writing these essays, the students were asked to discuss the kinds of experiences they had with people of other racial, ethnic, and religious groups; the derogatory phrases or stereotypes they heard, and the age at which they heard them; whether they had had the opportunity to know persons different from their own race, nationality, or religion since they started college; whether they ever invited people of a different ethnic, racial, or religious group to their homes as guests; whether they had people of different racial and/or ethnic groups as neighbors; and if they would be willing to date or even consider marrying a person of a different ethnic or racial group. These qualitative data were collected between 1985 and 1995. We call this study *Race and Ethnic Relations in the First Person* because respondents gave detailed "I" testimonies about their racial and ethnic experiences in their socialization process. In order to preserve anonymity of the respondents, phantom names are used in place of the personal names of the respondents and the colleges in which the surveys were conducted, but the stories are real.

Based on content analysis, the essays were categorized into five different themes. Each of these themes reflects the predominant social institution that most influenced or affected the respondents' perceptions, attitudinal changes, and opinions regarding persons of different ethnic and racial groups. The five categories are the basis for the chapters in the book. About ten essays were selected from each of the themes for inclusion in the book. The selection of an essay is based on the depth of coverage of the subject and the level of analytical rigor employed by the respondent.

RESEARCH SITES

Four colleges were the sites of the study. Site One is an inner-city community college located in a predominantly African American, Hispanic, Asiatic, and ethnic East European area. This college is part of a Metropolitan Community College (MCC) system with two campuses in the inner city and two campuses in the suburbs. We call this survey site Inner City Community College (ICCC), in part to reflect the geographic location of the college. Site Two is located in a progressive and affluent county that has the largest and most well funded community college system in the state, with a 98% White student body. We call this site Affluent County Community College (ACCC). Site Three is a parochial private college, which we dubbed Pay As You Earn (PAYE) liberal college. It is located in a small town in the outskirts of a large metropolitan area. Site Four is a state, four-year college located in a predominantly White small city. We call this site Normal College. The four sites provide a mix of students from various demographic, socioeconomic, and geographic backgrounds.

Site One

Inner City Community College (ICCC) and its sister campus, both members of the Metropolitan Community College (MCC) system, lie in the heart of Inner City in Dry County. They are adjacent to the ghetto. However, because educational opportunities favor Whites and are limited to the minorities who inhabit the ghetto in large numbers, the student populations at Inner City Community Colleges are predominantly White. These White students commute from suburban cities and towns in the Greater Metropolitan Area and sometimes as far as fifty miles away in the rural areas, which are also predominantly White. Two big cities in the Greater Metropolitan Area lie near Site One.

The number of residents in Inner City has remained stable, but some population characteristics have changed. A large Black population lives in this area over business houses, such as saloons and pool halls, which occupy the first floors of the buildings. This is said to be "a bad area" and according to one policeman: "Prostitution, drugs and violence go on there." There are also a growing number of refugees from third world countries housed in the area. Most of them have come from Ethiopia, Somalia, Uganda, Western Europe, Russia, Vietnam, South America, and elsewhere, between 1989 and 1991. Like the Jane Addams Hull House in Chicago during the tidal waves of immigration from Europe, the Catholic Center rehabilitates these refugees. As more and more people have come to live in the area, community facilities such as streets and sidewalks have deteriorated.

Since 1960, Inner City has maintained a population of about 22,000. The age characteristics of the population have shifted from an equal cross-section of age-groups (school aged, young adult, middle aged, and elderly) to a stronger concentration of school aged children (six years through nineteen years) and young adults (twenty years through thirty-four years). Racial characteristics have, over the years, changed from exclusively White to racially mixed. The Black population has increased from less than 1% in 1960 to over 35%, according to the 1990 Census of Population and Housing.

Racial and economic segregation characterize Inner City, and no meaningful action has been taken, nor has any significant progress been made, to reduce economic and social segregation. For instance, commercial opportunities are racially segregated and unequal. White business still thrives on the Country Club Plaza and is being encouraged to remain in the area. Both Whites and Blacks run separate offices in this area. There are Black joint stock companies composed of teachers, doctors, and lawyers in the Black community in this area. Even churches in this area are segregated. The Catholic church is dominant among Hispanics on the west side, while a Jewish temple lies on the south side. There are Black Muslims in this area too.

There are also "emergency" human service projects such as the Lighthouse, the Teenage Pregnancy Center, Ebony School for delinquent dropouts, and the W. E. B. Du Bois Learning Center—an alternative Afrocentric Curriculum School—that have developed to address the different ethnic problems in the area on a voluntary, self-help basis.

Progress has seemingly been made in school racial integration by the building of mandated magnet schools, but attracting Whites back into these inner-city schools remains an unrealized goal. Some African American parents have complained, in fact, that Inner City's desegregation effort and its emphasis on attracting White students to integrated magnet schools have ended up depriving Black students of improved educational opportunities. Some African Americans, especially the youth, think it is racist to be told that the only way Blacks will get a good education is if Whites are in the classroom.

The situation, with respect to higher education opportunities for disadvantaged youngsters growing up in Inner City, is not much different from their opportunities in primary and secondary education. Relatively few Inner City students are performing at an adequate level in public schools. The "average" pupil in Inner City schools reads at only the fifth- or sixth-grade level when entering high school and is inclined to drop out of school before receiving a high school diploma. The little evidence available indicates that fewer than 50% succeed in earning a high school diploma, due to the inadequate education provided in these predominantly low-income schools. Further, due to the financial burden of attending college, even those disadvantaged youth who have graduated from high school and have been able to proceed to college or university in the area have tended to falter by the wayside before their senior year.

It is probable that only a few of the disadvantaged youngsters who have grown up in Inner City have succeeded in obtaining a college degree and the job that usually comes with it. The U.S. Department of Education's National Center for Educational Statistics reported in October 1987 that 15% of all Blacks between the ages of thirteen and thirty-four in the metropolitan area were high school dropouts, compared with 11.3% of Whites.

Recognizing the fact that many of these young people are from socially disadvantaged minority groups, such as African American, Hispanic, Asiatic, and other ethnic groups, which also face discrimination in employment, it is easy to understand why many youths in Inner City are bitter, sadistic, and pessimistic toward the society in which they live. Because there are such large concentrations of low-income residents and students, it is very difficult to bring about much integration. The racial crisis has been compounded by economic and cultural differences. Among the few institutions that are leading the way to multicultural student bodies are Inner City Community College (ICCC) and its sister Metropolitan Community Colleges. This progress probably has come about because the ghetto forms the predominant catchment area for these campuses. However, the drama of racial tension is staged on these metropolitan campuses as well.

Race Relations in Site One

While Inner City is located near a variety of facilities and activities that support residents in the area, not all residents have access to the best there is. The transportation system provides access for area residents to an abundance of cultural, recreational, commercial, and institutional facilities. However, in this drive-yourself city, only those who can afford cars can conveniently go to these facilities. Those who do not have cars take the bus, one of the two public transport facilities (the other being the cab). However, the buses are still segregated, for they are dominated by minorities.

Inner City is comprised of a number of predominantly single-family residences, originally designed for middle-income families. However, many of the middle-income Whites have moved to the suburbs and left these homes to minorities and poor Whites who, nine times out of ten, need public assistance to pay rent. It is in this area that you find the homeless population. Many homes on the east side (the Black area) are also dilapidated.

Northwest, the Country Club Plaza, is a regional shopping center that provides general retail items, specialty goods, and recreation mainly for suburban Whites who come to display their wealth in expensive cars and ride in horse-drawn carriages. These horses are housed on the east side in a barn that used to be a business house before White flight started.

The Country Club Plaza, a multi-use shopping center that contains about 150 retail stores, 3 banks, office space, 2 luxury hotels, and many quality restaurants, is a White replica in a Black, poor White, and Mexican area. The Hospital, the Art

Gallery, the City Art Institute, and two four-year colleges are the major institutions in this area. The Mall, which includes a fountain and three parks, provides recreation space and playground facilities for people of all ages but not all races. A seventy-year-old Black lady who lived on the east side protested: "I do not want to go to do anything in the Country Plaza. Them Whites used not to allow us to go there when I was younger. I do not think they sincerely want us now." This view is held by many other Black people.

On the west side there is a combination of retail outlets, a dinner-playhouse, and a physical fitness facility. Two parks provide recreation and outdoor activity. A library and four schools are the major institutions that serve area residents. They, too, are visibly White or mixed, but they are dominated by Whites.

On the south side residents are also served by commercial activity. Moving in this direction, one comes upon a transition from Black to White residents. The Old Shopping Center is patronized mainly by Black people, while the New Shopping Center is patronized largely by Whites. There has been a scuffle or two in the New Shopping Center between Black and White patrons. All the Rent-A-Centers in this area are on the Black side, perhaps to target low-income Blacks and Whites who need to rent household amenities.

Another commercial area is on Noname Street and Godly Boulevard. There are four parks available in this area. Major institutions in this area are five fairly mixed but Black-dominated schools. There is also the Theological Seminary and a Research Hospital.

Although these northwestern, western, and southern boundaries are within reasonable distance of facilities that provide jobs, commercial activity, leisure opportunities, recreational space, and institutional services, minority residents of different races in Inner City have complained of institutional and *de facto* racism.

The transportation system may be thought to provide adequate circulation within the area and access to nearby facilities but, as we hinted earlier, increased public transportation may be needed. It is easy to get a bus within this area, but it is a nightmare if one wants to go to work or school further out in the suburbs, say in Affluent City, where the jobs are. The interior streets in Inner City are primarily local streets that circulate traffic within the area and feed into secondary or primary arterials. Three streets are designated secondary arterials and four are primary arterials. Integral to the transportation system are the public transit routes. There are only six routes that serve the area, leaving a gap in north and south bus service. Providing bus service in this area presents a problem because of the street system. There is only one complete through street and many streets are too narrow. The topography is hilly and may present a problem during bad weather, especially in the winter.

The cheapest transportation is available only for the elderly and the handicapped through the city's Share-A-Fare program. Persons sixty-five years of age or older or those physically disabled can travel up to a distance of four miles for fifty cents. Vehicles used must be authorized by the city. The people most hurt by the transportion system are those of college or working age who could venture into the suburbs to get jobs or go to better colleges such as Affluent County Community College, but cannot get there unless they own a vehicle. The Business College tries to bus Inner City students to Affluent City, but no other college extends this service to Inner City residents.

Site Two

Site two is a rapidly growing suburban complex and serves as the showpiece of American progress, especially to its inhabitants who proudly point out that Affluent County is one of the richest counties in the United States. This county is the home of the large, mushrooming, and steadily expanding Affluent County Community College, which is located in Affluent City. Affluent County is also home to The Business College (TBC).

Affluent County's socioeconomic and educational affluence contrasts sharply with Inner City's socioeconomic and educational deprivation. It is a complex mixture of urban and rural areas. The northeastern corner of the county is densely populated, due to suburban growth from Metropolis. Affluent County began the twentieth century with about 18,000 people. It grew slowly until World War II, reaching a population of about 33,000 by 1940. After the war suburban expansion quadrupled the population so that by 1960 a total of 143,792 people lived in the county. The 1960s saw continued growth as 42,000 more people were added—a 30% increase due to White flight from surrounding cities. Since 1970, the population has increased to a 1990 population of about 300,000, ranking it the second most populous county in the state. By the year 2000, it is expected that about 375,000 people will reside in Affluent County. This population is predominantly White. As the county has grown, the population center has shifted south and west.

Affluent City is one of fourteen contiguous cities in Affluent County, with few signs to indicate the passage from one city to the other. Street names do not change from city to city, and the characteristics of adjacent areas are usually so similar that the cities seem to flow into each other, thus constituting one affluent sprawling White suburbia.

The school district here is considered to be the richest in the metropolitan area. Here, and elsewhere in other school districts, funds determine the quality of education and educational equity. The schools here, including Affluent County Community College, have the following funding sources: the *ad valorem* property tax, state income tax, motor vehicle tax, and the state equalization tax, which is collected by the County Treasurer and returned to the district. In addition, a special levy is made for capital improvements. This method of funding puts high-income Affluent County ahead of counties that have a poorer tax base and lower-income minority populations in large numbers.

The State Power Equalization method of school financing, which was passed by the 1973 legislature for the purpose of equalizing the per-pupil cost of education throughout the state, seems to benefit the White pupils in Affluent City more than it benefits the residents in Inner City, simply because minorities, due to segregated residences, do not have full access to schools in Affluent County. "Local effort" (the amount a school district can raise from its own *ad valorem* levy, an amount based on assessed property valuation) is taken into account in allocating equalization aid. This consideration again favors the affluent White school districts like Affluent County more than it does Inner City districts.

Another part of the local effort that favors affluent districts is the state income tax raised in a given district; 20% of state income tax collected from a district is returned to the district in the form of state revenue sharing. The cost per pupil is then "equalized" by varying degrees of state aid from the general fund. A school district with high income or high valuation will receive less state aid, but in these days of budget cuts, when all government programs are gasping for breath, poor districts suffer more than rich ones because rich districts can use local funds to bale themselves out of hard times. The rich district is, of course, ahead and funding of schools is what has made a big difference between Affluent County and Inner City schools.

Race Relations in Site Two

In Affluent City the red carpet is reluctantly rolled up for people of color, especially African Americans, Hispanics, and Asian immigrants who look for residences there. The real estate agents try to steer them away from the most exclusive neighborhoods. Those people of color who have broken through encounter a brand of racism that is very rebellious—such as the short temper of a store clerk or the fact that nobody asks a Black teenager to the high school prom.

One retired Mayor, who stirred local criticism and national attention in the late 1960s by helping the first Black family settle in Affluent City, says it is vastly different today, but adds: "Of course we have an awful long way to go, but I don't think you can force it."

A check of government agencies suggests that while efforts are made to include Black people in the work force, they often make up only a small percentage. As of early summer 1990 the Affluent County Sheriff's Department employed 6 Black officers out of 204 applicants; police departments in two cities in Affluent County, with a combined force of about 85, employed no Black officers. Only a few Black people hold elected positions in Affluent County municipalities.

This contrasts sharply with Inner City, where the Mayor is Black. Of the roughly 1,900 teachers in the Affluent County School District in 1990, 28 were Black. One of sixteen central office administrators was Black as were two of fifty-seven principals. No Black people sit on school boards. In Affluent County Community College, between 1985 and 1990 there were less than five Black faculty and staff: one was a coach, one was a business professor, one woman worked in continuing education, and one was an African exchange instructor. This again contrasts sharply with Inner City Community College and Sister Pioneer Campuses, where one Black woman has served as president, two Black men have served as Dean of

Instruction and Dean of Student Services, respectively and Black men and women serve in all sections of the college. The Assistant President of Inner City Community College, who in 1991 became Dean of Instruction, is a Black woman. In Site Two no more than sixty of the ten thousand businesses in the county have Black owners, according to estimates of the Black Chamber of Commerce of Greater Metropolitan Area. Officials in Affluent County attribute such figures to the low number of Black residents but the Equal Employment Opportunity Commission (EEOC) would prefer that employers achieve a racial mix that reflects the entire Metropolitan area, which is 13% Black. This shows a miserable performance of affirmative action.

Site Three

Pay As You Earn (PAYE) liberal college is in Little Dixie (dubbed Cow City), a small city north of Rural County, which lies north of a large metropolitan area. In 1992 Rural County had a total population of about 61,000 people, with a density of 147 persons per square mile. Of these, 26% were under eighteen and 9% were sixty-five and over. Educationally, about 88% of Little Dixie's population has completed high school and 26% are college graduates, in contrast with Affluent County where 93% are high school graduates, and 41% have earned a bachelor's degree or higher. The 1993 median household income of Rural County residents after taxes was about $38,000 in contrast with the $49,000 median household income in Affluent County. In Rural County some 6% of the residents and 4% of the families live below the poverty level. The unemployment rate in Rural County is about 6%, compared to 4% in Affluent County. In Rural County 33% of the residents live in the rural areas on their farms, 1% in group quarters, and 89% in single-family residences.

Race Relations in Site Three

There are 95% White residents, 2% African Americans, 1% Asian and Pacific Islanders, 0.4% American Indians, Eskimos, and Aleut, and about 3% Hispanics of any race in Rural County. Little Dixie, the headquarters of Rural County, is a community of ethnic, social class, and racial neighborhoods. The northeastern area (dubbed Little Italy) is one such neighborhood; it is made up of Italian and Catholic middle-class households, and with no Blacks whatsoever living in the area. North central of Little Dixie is another neighborhood, characterized as WASP. However, though some of its houses are new, its property values are lower than in Affluent County.

In Little Dixie, there are also company houses that accommodate blue and white collar employees of a large Airline. Little Dixie also has single-family older residences. The people there are friendly and are proud of their small college—Pay As You Earn. There are a lot of retired and older people in Little Dixie, although younger people started moving into the area in the last ten years. Little shops have been opening up and closing, but more and more, shops are becoming secure in Little Dixie. There is a strong awareness of isolated racial, ethnic, and social-class pockets in the area. Residents express standard stereotypical and prejudicial views and beliefs regarding these neighborhoods. For example; "Little Dixie—very anti-Black, maybe democratic but very conservative, feel apart from the inner city." And there are stereotypes too; "Northeast—Polish and people who have no ambition."

Despite these racial stereotypes, Pay As You Earn College tries to reach out and recruit minority students from Inner City. In fact, most of the federal grants that come to the county are Urban Grant Program funds meant for disadvantaged students. This might account for the reason Pay As You Earn College has an outreach center in Inner City, where its professors give classes to students who otherwise could not afford transportation or could not stand the racial attitudes in Little Dixie.

Site Four

Normal College is one of several colleges in a statewide university system located in Lacustrine City. The college has a student population of about 11,000, of which 500 are minority students. There are also 600 faculty and academic staff, of which less than 1% are minority. Although college officials have over the years made efforts to increase the size of minority faculty and students at the college, not much success has been achieved in this regard. Most Black students come from the largest city in the state, which has a large minority population. Many of those who come to Normal College drop out or transfer to other schools because they feel unwelcome and alienated in conservative and predominantly White Lacustrine City in which Normal College is located. It is safe to say that Blacks are still an exotic breed in Lacustrine City and most people in the city have never had contact with a Black person. The largest minority group is Asian. This is because of the influx of Hmong refugees from Asia, who migrated to the United States to flee persecution in their homeland for helping the United States during the Vietnam War.

Lacustrine City is located at the confluence of two rivers that empty into two lakes. With the city's convenient location on sources of water, it attracted several pioneer traders and explorers who settled in the area. The city developed as a result of the lumber industry. The early settlers were Poles, Danes, Germans, Welsh, and Irish who all came to work in the lumber mills. Later, as rivers became less important as a means of transportation, Lacustrine City's economy changed with the times and the city diversified its economic base to include industries in cloth making and vehicle manufacturing. Today Lacustrine City has a population of about 60,000. A large segment of the city's population is employed in manufacturing and blue collar work as machine operators, assemblers, and precision workers. Surrounding Lacustrine City is a large, rural population engaged primarily in dairy farming. The educational system is one of the best in the state, but it is also reported that some 5,000 residents are functionally illiterate.

Lacustrine City's economy is integrated with the rest of the cities that make up the River Valley region. There are about eighty-four smaller towns in this region with a combined population of about half a million people. Most of the students at Normal College are drawn from this region.

Race Relations in Site Four

Because Lacustrine City is predominantly White, there is no spatial segregation by race, and no ethnic segregation is visible in the city either. However, the city has grown and expanded north and west leaving the central city, which habors the older residential neighborhoods to lower-income households and recent third-world immigrants. This is where you find the city's three public housing developments. However, unlike other cities, these buildings cater primarily to the elderly, who make up about 98% of the residents. The rest of the population in the public housing projects consists of persons with disabilities. The westward expansion of the city threatens the very fabric of the central city, and efforts to attract high-income households back to the central city have not succeeded.

While no racial tensions currently exist in the city, the early years of city formation were rancorous. There was considerable mistrust between German and Irish groups, between Protestants and Catholics, and between "lowland" Germans and "highland" Germans. This animosity was so great that a local historian observed that it became a yearly tradition to close off one of the residential streets in the city to allow for fistfights between the groups. There was also considerable conflict between residents north of the Eagle River, which divides the city into two, and those south of the river.

Although there were some ninety-eight Black residents in the city around 1910, there were no reports of any major Black and White conflicts, although one 89-year-old woman, a long-term resident of the city, said that a Black man tried to date a White woman and was run out of the city in the 1930s. Today, there is no Black neighborhood in Lacustrine City as many of the Black residents have migrated out of the city. Although statistics indicate a large Black population still resides in the city, this is misleading because most of them are in the three state correction facilities. Corrections is one of the fastest growing industries in Lacustrine City. Although residents in Lacustrine City benefit from the jobs that come with the expansion of these correctional institutions, some are wary that further expansion of these facilities might encourage an influx, and settlement, of relatives of inmates to the area.

One of the most notable events in race relations in the city is what has become known as "Black Thursday" because of student riots that took place in Normal College on the 21st of November 1968. On this fateful day, Black students who had earlier presented a list of demands to the Chancellor of the college and received no immediate response, staged a riot at the college that resulted in the destruction of college property. The students' demands included the hiring of Black professors, the implementation of courses in Black culture, and the establishment of an African American Cultural center. The riot reverberated to the community at large and even received national attention. This led to the expulsion of several Black students from the college.

Following the disturbance, a faculty-student committee was set up to study the students' requests and to make recommendations to the Board of Regents. While a Black Center has since been established at the college, progress on the other requests by the students has been slow. Today, Lacustrine City and Normal College exhibit no visible signs of racial animosity.

SUMMARY

These four communities are the social laboratories from which subjects were drawn for this study. While the opinions and life histories of the students may not be representative of a cross section of the U.S. population, the stories enable us to better understand the individual and personal circumstances that help to shape opinions about "the other" race or ethnic group. Drawn from different demographic, geographic, ethnic, and racial backgrounds, the stories help to enrich our understanding of the racial mosaic in the United States and how we can begin to address the fears and obstacles that keep us apart.

OUTLINE OF THE REST OF THE BOOK

In this chapter we discussed the rationale for the book, the research methodology, and the context within which the study took place. In the next chapter—chapter two—we examine a collection of essays by people who were overawed and traumatized as a result of an event or events that awakened them to the prevalence of racism and discrimination, which they had previously viewed to be unimportant in their social relations with other ethnic and racial groups. These essays, like the rest of the essays in the book, show that social institutions in the United States help to cultivate racial and ethnic attitudes in people.

The essays in chapter three show children's convergent and divergent reactions to parental racial and ethnic attitudes, especially in the formative years of the children. Some essays show that children whose parents had positive attitudes went on to exhibit similar attitudes themselves until some episode either enhanced their openness to those different from them or made them change to a negative attitude. Other essays reveal that while few children blindly followed their parents' negative attitudes, a greater number of children negated their parents' stance, sometimes at the risk of being disowned.

Chapter four is a collection of essays that illuminates the opportunities that people have to interact with those of diverse ethnic and racial backgrounds at work and at play. However, while some of the essays show that positive interaction breaks stereotypes and improves relationships, other essays indicate that negative interaction at work and play may perpetuate stereotypes and lead to racial and ethnic conflict.

In chapter five the essays show that the college environment, in a number of ways, provides a unique opportunity for people to get to meet others of different ethnic and racial backgrounds. Some of the essays reveal that this interaction leads some to modify their opinions about persons of other races and ethnic groups. For others, the interaction confirms their worst fears of other racial and ethnic groups. Just like in the workplace, some find the interaction with people of different backgrounds liberating while others are disillusioned by it.

A collection of the life stories of immigrants is shared in chapter six. The essays enable us to make a comparison between the accounts of immigrants and those of native-born Americans in their conceptions of ethnic and racial differences. The reader is also treated to a sampling of some of the racial, ethnic, and religious problems prevalent in other countries of the world.

In the concluding chapter we reflect on the stories in the book under the five themes and discuss the lessons we can draw from them to better understand race and ethnic relations in the United States. We also offer suggestions for improving intercultural understanding.

2

Innocence Lost

The essays in this chapter are the stories of persons whose views about the world changed as a result of racist or ethnic-related incidents. From their stories, we learn about the disturbing effects that racist attitudes and behaviors have on the psyche of the innocent and how this changes the worldview of those who are impacted by these incidents. In a number of ways, the essays also confirm the belief that the acquisition of racist behavior is not inborn but that it is developed through a process of socialization. Through the authors' stories we take a walk through the home, the workplace, the school, and the neighborhood in urban and rural America. Here we see the relations between White and Black America, Hispanic and Asian families, and even recent immigrants, as they address some of their worst fears of "the other." Together, the essays remind us of the role that adults play in the acculturation of children and in shaping their perceptions and attitudes, especially regarding people of a different race or ethnic background. We are also reminded in these essays that it is the inaction of those who should have acted and the silence of those who should have spoken up that has led to the perpetuation of racism and prejudice in our society. The essays point to the equanimity with which children view the world and suggest that, perhaps, we all need to be children again, at least in our thoughts, in order that we might live peaceably together. Here now are the stories of the innocent.

I DIDN'T KNOW MY GUEST WAS THE WRONG COLOR

When I was four years old, my parents moved us to the suburbs so that we would have a better home, a better education, better grammar, better everything. Their intentions were the best in the world. They did it for us, for me and my sisters. My parents worked very hard and sacrificed to make this dream of theirs come true. Suburbia was a magic word in 1958, and our young family was like many other White, lower-middle-class, Protestant families who thought the suburbs were the end-all of the standard of living. So we moved to our new house and that's where

I grew up. My parents always worked hard to give me and my sisters a good upbringing. I appreciate all of their efforts now—but I didn't always back then.

I was the baby of the family. I have two older sisters. I was lonesome often when I was little because there was such a gap in our ages. I was always looking for someone to play with. I was very friendly.

I created quite a panic in our house one day. I threw my mother for a loop and put panic in her heart I'm sure—all because I brought home a guest who was the wrong color. It happened when I was in the second grade. I met a new friend at school, a little girl who I thought had the prettiest, smooth, brown skin. I was fascinated by her. We came skipping in the house, hand in hand, smiling, happy, and chattering away. I didn't know then that what I had done was something my family considered to be unspeakable. Where I came from, there were no people of color. They weren't good enough to live where I lived—this is what I grew up hearing. I didn't know that day that my poor mother would have hell to pay if our father came home and found a Black child in his house. This was a serious no-no.

Now I can look back and see the awkward position in which I had put my mother. My parents were both very prejudiced against any people of color or anyone who was different from them. If you didn't look like us, talk like us, dress like us, and live like us, then that meant, in my father's eyes, that you must not be as good as us. So here was my mother on one hand wanting to encourage me to have friends, but on the other hand dreading the thought of my father finding out about this little girl being in our house. I remember her telling me it was time for my friend to be getting home. She told me I could walk the girl up to the corner, but when I got back home my mother just simply said, "Don't ever bring her here again."

I didn't understand my father's prejudice but I didn't question it either. His hatred toward Blacks was the greatest. Next in line were Asians, then Italians. How many times did I hear my father say that Blacks were only good for two things: sports and music, and nothing else. And that all Italians were hotheads, not to be trusted. For years as his child, I listened and I accepted his views and his opinions. I didn't realize that someday I might develop my own thoughts and feelings. At that time in my life, my father's word was all there was.

When I was eighteen, I went to nursing school at University Medical Center (UMC). There, for the first time in my life, I was among all different kinds of people, and I found out right away that I enjoyed being around so many different kinds of people. There I found out that I was no better, no smarter, no prettier than any of the other girls. I realized that I could get along with people with different skin color and different cultural backgrounds.

After I graduated from LPN training, I continued to work at UMC. I was a staff nurse on a large internal medical unit. We had all kinds of patients, with all kinds of illnesses. There were diabetics, people with heart problems, cancer, intestinal problems, and dialysis patients. We had many older patients on our floor—they were my favorite to take care of. I have always felt at ease around elderly people—I like to help them and listen to them.

While I was working all those years, I was very happy. I loved the work. I loved the hospital. I loved being there. UMC became my home away from home; my second family. I was dedicated to my work there. I met my husband at UMC. We worked together on the same floor. My sons were born at UMC. After my second son was born, it got hard for me to give as much of my time and energy to working as I had always done. By that time I had worked on the same floor, at the same job, for ten years. I had just about reached the end of my stress level. I suffered from what is called "burn-out" among health care workers. I needed a change. I had let myself become much too emotionally involved with my patients and my job over the years. I felt worn down and ineffective. So I quit working to stay home with my family. I ended up staying home for six years taking care of my babies.

I am thirty-seven years old now and in many ways I feel like I'm just starting to grow up. My mother used to say, "The older I get, the more I realize how much I don't know about life." I always thought she sounded silly saying such a thing. Now I understand exactly what she meant. I realize now there is so much I don't know. My goal is to become a stronger person—stronger mentally, spiritually, and emotionally—so that I will be able to contribute something worthwhile in my lifetime. I am past that part of my life where I only thought about myself and what I wanted. Now I am starting to become more aware of the world around me.

The man I married is of a different race than me. When I married him, I believed with all my heart that my strength and my faith and my love would help us to overcome any prejudice we might face from our society and our own families. I think when two people of different color marry, they need some measure of extra inner strength and dedication because in our society, they will certainly run into extra obstacles as a couple and as a family. Ideally, we should not let ourselves be affected by negative outside forces, but in my own experience, I found this easier said than done.

Twelve years ago when I married my husband, I couldn't foresee the problems that might come down the road. All I knew was that I was in love and I felt sure that everything would go smoothly for us. But there have been problems. One of my greatest concerns now is for my children. How will they be treated by society and by their peers? Of course, I wish I could shield them from any kind of pain, and it angers me to know that they could very likely have some difficulties in life because they are "mixed." My aim is to instill in them a deep and true sense of love, self-worth, and identity. These values will give them strength as they go through life. I have a friend who is of the Bahai faith. She told me that children born to two different races are special in God's eyes. I wish more people felt this way.

To summarize, I would like to say a few more things about prejudice. I hear so many times people say, "I'm not prejudiced. No, not me. I don't care what color you are—it doesn't matter to me one bit that you're different from me. Oh no, I'm not prejudiced." Well, I found it necessary to put the whole issue in perspective. The word "prejudice" has become a dirty word in this country. I think it has been taken to extremes. If we are truthful about it, we should be able to look at a person of a different skin color and say, "Yes, you are different than me in that respect." What is wrong with admitting to that difference? We shouldn't have to be ashamed about it or get defensive about it. Just because there is a difference doesn't have to make it a negative thing, does it? My father was openly prejudiced. He didn't care who knew it—in fact he acted proud to display it. He thought it was his God-given right to feel superior because he was a White man. My mother always was, and still is, prejudiced. I can't point my finger at her and blame her for it. She was brought up to believe certain things about certain people. She never questioned her feelings, they were just natural to her. My point is that I think we are all prejudiced to a degree. It has taken me a long time to be able to truthfully admit this. I just don't see how or why we should have to deny that there are differences among people. I personally have a long way to go before I completely understand this problem and resolve my feelings about it.

I may die before I figure it all out, but I feel strongly that the similarities that all people share on the inside should outweigh the differences of our outer appearances.

EVERYONE BLAMED THE 220 PROGRAM

As a child in elementary school, I do not recall any negative comments made by schoolmates, teachers, or my parents toward people of different racial and ethnic backgrounds. My best friend was African American, so that may be why I did not hear some of the comments, if there were any. During my middle school years, I moved to a bigger town, a suburb of Milwaukee. The school I went to had all White children attending. The attitudes of my classmates were unreal to me. I couldn't believe they would talk bad about a specific group of people without ever meeting them. I figured out that the reason they must have felt this way was because of what their parents told them and what they saw on the news.

During my high school years in that same town, the school board introduced a program called the 220 program. This program bused African American students from Milwaukee to our school and some students from our school to Milwaukee public schools. With much opposition from the community, the school board allowed the program to begin. I can still remember the first few days the African American students were there. The tension in the school was high, not only from the students, but also from the teachers. No one knew how to react. Most of the White students isolated the Black students and kept them from feeling welcome. They called them derogatory names, and picked fights with them. Every afternoon we would have at least one fight between a White student and a Black student. The administration didn't help matters when they didn't address the problems that were occurring. They never wanted to admit that there was a racial problem in our school. When anything in the school went wrong, everyone blamed the 220 students.

I was friends with some of the 220 students. They were great people. I tried to get them together with some of my White friends. Some of them then began to accept the Black students and some wondered why I would hang around them. The objectives of busing students to different schools are to provide equal educational opportunities and to reduce racial prejudice through interaction. Although this may happen at other schools, it didn't happen at mine. Nor did the school board or faculty try to redirect the program so it would. All it did was to intensify racial tensions and help continue a controversy for the past five years in the community. The values my parents instilled in me early on in life helped me ignore the negative comments and made me able to meet some terrific students.

Since I started at Normal College, I haven't had a great deal of contact with people of different racial or ethnic backgrounds. There isn't a great deal of diversity at this university. I have had some contacts with different cultures. I do attend programs and even help present some on different cultures and religions, so I can better enrich my life and come to know more about other people.

My parents taught me the value of being nice to everyone, no matter what race or religion they were. They told me I needed to treat people as I would like to be treated. To this day I still carry their message and I am glad I do. The only negative comments I remember hearing at an early age were from my grandparents. They stated that African Americans were bad and dirty people, that they would steal from you and hurt you, so we needed to be careful when they were around us. These statements made it confusing for a while, until my parents sat us down and ensured us that they were not bad, my grandparents had just said that because that was how they were taught by their parents.

It is said that prejudice is a learned phenomenon and is transmitted from generation to generation through socialization. I feel this is true to some extent. I have seen many prejudiced children who have received their hatred for others from their parents. But I have also seen a few who have received this information from friends. Children, especially adolescents, will follow what their peers are saying or doing to fit in.

I have had people of different racial and ethnic backgrounds in my home, as my neighbors, as my classmates, and as fellow employees. All of these encounters with people have helped me accept differences in other people. I would consider marrying a man of another racial or ethnic background. If I love that person it would not matter what race or religion he may be on the outside. I look to love someone who is special and beautiful on the inside. I feel, as human service workers, we need to improve these situations. Each person in the world provides something special that no one else can. People need to learn to be accepting of others, even if they do not agree with their lifestyle, and that learning starts with us.

MY HUSBAND, THE GOOD SAMARITAN

The story of the Good Samaritan is very familiar to me. Since I was a small child, I've heard the story time and time again. I've grown to hold the main principle of the parable important in my Christian life. I give freely to friends and loved ones in need. I always believed that "all men are created equal." Little did I know one day this value I hold so true would be tested.

I heard my husband talking with someone in the living room. I glanced at the alarm clock by our bed. It read 2:30 A.M. He had arrived home later than usual from his evening shift at work. I thought probably he brought a co-worker home to visit for a while. I drifted back off to sleep. The gentle touch of my husband's hand on my shoulder awakened me a few moments later. "Kathy, I'm moving Julie to Matt's room. I've brought someone home with me. He needs a place to sleep." "Who is it, John?" "It's a guy I picked up on the highway. He has nowhere to go. I'll talk to you about it more in the morning." I could feel my husband's determination to have this man stay even though I felt uncomfortable about the situation.

Down the hall through the opened bedroom door, I glanced to take a look at the stranger. There stood a tall Black man wearing a T-shirt and shorts. It appeared that it had been some time since he'd showered or shaved. My uneasiness grew as I tiptoed back to my bed. I heard my husband orient him to the room he'd be staying in for the night. John then said good night to the man and came to bed. My husband said nothing as he crawled into bed next to me. He just kissed me good night. I had several questions that couldn't wait till morning. "He's not a paranoid schizophrenic that's going to kill us all in the middle of the night, is he?" John turned over and said, "Kathy, don't be ridiculous. He's a guy who's experienced some bad luck. His mother and father are both dead and when he came home from college to live with his sister, his sister moved her boyfriend in and him out. Now, go to sleep. It's going to be fine." With that statement, he gave me a kiss on the cheek and rolled back over. I could hear his snoring within minutes. I restlessly attempted to find sleep but it would not come. Finally, at 5:30 A.M., I got up, made a pot of coffee, and started getting ready for the day. My daughters got up later and we all went to school as usual. My husband and the stranger slept soundly when I left.

I returned home from school later that day sure that John and the stranger would be gone. I was wrong. I found them sitting at the kitchen table visiting. They both stood to their feet when I walked through the door. "Kathy, I'd like for you to meet a friend of mine," my husband said. "Ron, this is my wife Kathy, Kathy this is Ron Washington." "Nice to meet you, Ron," I replied. Ron then shook my hand. "Nice to meet you, ma'am. I really appreciate you and your husband's generosity." John then summoned me to the next room. "I've made arrangements to send Ron to San Francisco by bus today at 4:00 P.M. You'll need to take him to the bus depot because I have to go to work. I've taken $200.00 out of the bank to pay for the bus ticket. Also, you'll need to give him $20.00 for food. It's a forty-seven-hour bus ride," John whispered. "Why is he going to San Francisco? Can't he find someone around here to move in with? How are we going to afford this?" I questioned. "He's moving in with a close friend. There is no one for him here in Inner City." I felt my first emotion of uneasiness shift to anger. I didn't want to make a scene so I said "OK" to the situation and went back to the kitchen. My husband said his good-byes and left for work. I fumed on the inside. How could he leave me here with some stranger off the street? Isn't he worried about me? Didn't I have enough to do without taking care of someone I didn't know from Adam? I made small conversation with Ron hoping my anger and frustration didn't show through. Through the conversation I found that Ron was a senior at a State University, attending on a full scholastic scholarship. His major was industrial engineering with a minor in music.

Within an hour my daughters returned home from school. I worried about their reaction to this stranger. They took to him from the beginning. The girls danced, sang, and played the piano for him. Ron joined in and acted like he was loving every minute. My youngest asked Ron if he wanted to play Nintendo with her. He consented wholeheartedly. She then took him by the hand and led him back to her room where the Nintendo was. As I watched them, my heart sank with shame. Instantly, my own attitude toward this situation was revealed to me. Here a little one, untainted by the world's prejudice and cruelty, showed genuine hospitality and concern for this stranger.

Soon the time came for taking Ron to the bus station. As we said good-bye, my emotions were mixed. I felt relieved things would get back to normal, but I also felt guilt over my unsympathetic attitude toward this incident.

If I were faced with this situation again, or a similar situation today, I'm not sure how I would react. Would I take the stranger in and take care of his needs like the Good Samaritan? Or would I be too concerned over my unfounded fears and pass on the other side as did the priest? Perhaps, like the Levite, I would feel no common bond with the stranger, therefore, it would not be my responsibility to take time out of my busy schedule. Hopefully I've learned to be more like the Good Samaritan. If I have learned from this experience, I will follow the biblical principle, "Dear children, let us not love with words or tongue but with actions and with truth" (1 John 3:18).

YOU DON'T MAKE FRIENDS WITH BLACK BOYS

My history of racism is very simple. There were no Blacks, Hispanics, Native Americans, or Asian children in my school, church, or neighborhood. We did have one Indian man as a neighbor but he moved within two years. If I remember right, he moved because he was discriminated against. As a child I did not know why there was no one of any other color in my life. I didn't ask, and no one even mentioned it. I did know different colored skins existed because I saw pictures of them. I also know that I didn't call a Black man a "nigger" because it wasn't nice.

When I was in the ninth grade, I finally met a Black person. There were two Black girls and one Black boy who went to my school. Both girls were in my choir class and the boy was in my band class. I was acquainted with them but we were never best friends. I don't remember anyone ever telling me not to make friends with them. I didn't want to be their friend because they were different from me.

Usually best friends have a lot in common, and I couldn't see myself playing makeup with a Black person.

The Black boy who was in my band class liked me. Before we met in band class he saw me at the first school dance. I had won a dancing contest, and he was impressed. He also thought I had a beautiful smile. In our school we had phone books with all the students' home phone numbers and addresses in them—they don't have them any more in public schools because of the potential for crime. He started calling me every night, and we became pretty good friends. Then I learned my first lesson in prejudice. When my mother found out a Black boy was calling me, she about went through the roof. "You don't make friends with Black boys. You tell him not to talk to you anymore because you don't talk to Black boys." When I refused to tell him what she had told me to tell him, she called his parents. I never saw him in my class again. He was still in my class, we just never made eye contact again.

During high school my friends and I used the phrase "There is a difference between a 'nigger' and a Black person." Niggers smell, use bad English, act like a street person, and usually have very dark skin. The only difference between a White person and a Black person is the skin color. For a Black person to be accepted at our high school he or she had to act and talk like a White. He or she had to be smart and athletic. This statement was also viewed as true by the Black people in my school. We did not have any niggers in our school.

When I was twenty-one, I worked with Blacks at a collection agency. This was my first contact with a large number of colored people. We had both types, Blacks and niggers. Because of their ability to "talk shit," they were all very intelligent and good at their jobs. I was intrigued with how they talked on the phone to debtors. They could change their voices and mannerism in speaking to suit the characteristics of the person with whom they were speaking. There was no prejudice in the workplace. We were all there to do a job and team work was a necessity. We didn't have time to worry about what color a person was because each and everyone of us had a job to do and needed the others to achieve the organization's goal.

I worked at a different collection agency for a couple of months. At this job I had a Black supervisor. She and I did not get along. The problem was her prejudice toward Whites, not my prejudice toward Blacks. She had the notion that every White person hated her because she was Black. She overcompensated for this insecurity. Her orders were short and insensitive. She was very quick to blame without researching to find where and how a mistake was made, and when I took it upon myself to find out where the mistakes came from, I found that she was making more of them. She asked several times if I had a problem with her. Even though I told her no, she was still intimidated by me. A girlfriend of mine also worked under her. The outcome of the situation was inevitable. I left the company. My friend was taken out of her supervision, and debates to fire the Black woman began. I don't know if she was ever fired or if she quit because they were worried that she would try to sue on grounds of discrimination.

Since I've been here at TBC, I have noticed that there are a lot of Blacks here. I am a little shocked. I was not expecting this many Blacks. I had assumed that because this college was in the heart of Affluent County there would be few Blacks. Don't misunderstand me, I am not disappointed. I have met and become friends with a few Blacks. I am very picky when it comes to choosing my friends and as I grow older, I am learning that being Black is making a lesser difference. I don't think I will ever be able to tolerate a nigger, but I think that I could become friends with a Black.

I DON'T TRUST MY CAUCASIAN FRIENDS

As a child growing up in a dominant White community, I have experienced harsh racism and prejudice. This is not to say all Caucasians were that way, but most of them were. Those whom I have had an opportunity to get acquainted with became good friends with me. Even though we were friends, there was still a gap between the two cultures—my culture and the dominant White culture. I was eager to learn their culture, and they were cautious to learn my culture. The reason for their behavior is because of the stereotypes that they hear. A good example is when I first invited my Caucasian friend to eat with us. He was cautious because he heard that Asian people eat dogs. This is a typical reason why I never become close friends with the majority of Caucasians that I meet, because they judge people by what they hear. I feel that they don't have the heart to appreciate my culture in depth. Therefore, I don't have the heart to trust and appreciate their culture in depth either. Most of my close friends throughout my childhood were mainly minorities. The reason I say this is because some cultures have similarities and most, if not all, have been through the same experiences. I feel that there is more unity between minorities. This was my belief until later. As I became older I began to see and experience segregation between races, especially in college. Everyone is in their own group and is shy or not willing to open up and learn about other cultures besides theirs. For example, minority clubs do not support each other, but rather each group supports their own club and are afraid or shy to interact with others.

This is also illustrative of my childhood. During my childhood we all got along and had the sense of belonging, and as we got older, we tended to hang around our own kind for security, identity, and a sense of belonging. A perfect example is the relationship between me and my Puerto Rican friend. We grew up together and shared each other's culture but as we grew older we started talking about how each one's culture was better than the other's. These situations that I just explained are my personal experiences and could be different in another environment. For example, I don't know what it would be like if I lived in a predominantly Black or Hispanic community.

I enjoy learning about other cultures because they are very interesting to me. In a way my family is like a melting pot. My sisters-in-law are African American and Mexican, my brother-in-law is Chinese, and my soon to be brother-in-law is Puerto

Rican. Besides my family, I have a Caucasian friend and a Puerto Rican friend, who are like brothers to me, because we grew up together in the same neighborhood. I have also been learning how to speak Spanish in order to communicate with my Spanish friends. As much as I commit myself to learning their culture, they are just as committed to learning mine. A few of my friends can now speak a little Hmong.

In terms of religion, my family was brought up Catholic. I have not experienced anything wrong with being Catholic, except with those who are racist and yet proclaim themselves as believers of God. We once had a neighbor who went to the same church as we did, but who did not allow his children to come close to us, and once called the police to give a false accusation that he saw marijuana in my dad's station wagon. The police came in search of the illegal drug and were very disappointed to find that it was only a vegetable plant. It made me angry—how can people like that believe in God, when they do not exercise his words? With my religious values and the way my parents raised me, I have an open mind toward many things, whether it be race or religion.

I DENIED WHO I WAS

I grew up in a predominantly Caucasian community. The time that I was growing up and attending elementary school, the Hmong community was very small and also there was not much diversity in Lacustrine City. I remember there were at least two other Hmong students going to my school.

As a child, I never knew how to judge people by their color or culture. Everyone who wanted to be friends with me, I accepted. There was a time that made me feel separated from the other kids and that was when Greg, a boy whom I went to school with, wouldn't let me play with them because I was different (not White). He told the other girlfriends of mine that they shouldn't play with me because I was Chinese. He didn't even know my culture. That hurt me so badly. I realized then that because of my cultural differences I wasn't accepted. Although I was hurt by him, my friends didn't shy away. They still liked me. Partly because of this incident, I began to deny who I was and ignore my culture. I wanted to be accepted in the White community and the only way was to act and do everything like they did. I smoked, drank, hung around them, and dressed like them. I was very embarrassed to bring people to my house because a lot of my friends were rich and we were poor. I didn't want people to not talk to me because my family was poor. I hated my childhood because I lived as a different person. It was me on the outside but inside was someone else. That's how prejudice influenced my childhood. It wasn't until high school that I went to a minority conference and discovered myself, and when I did I was so happy and proud of who I was that no one could hurt me again.

During this time, my family was very open minded. They never told me to hang around just Hmong girls; they let me play with just about everyone. They were just concerned that I would forget my own culture. I consider myself very lucky to have a great family. We are a very diverse family. My sister-in-law is African American, I am marrying a Puerto Rican, and my second oldest brother is marrying a Mexican. I think my parents are positive role models for me, and they opened my mind and heart to accept every culture. My fiance is Pentecostal and my family is Catholic. They are not worried about that, as long as he and I share spiritual belief together.

As I reached my freshman year at Normal College, I shared the same room with one of the girls from my school. I used to cook Hmong food, and she would come in and ask me, "What is that stinky smell?" I asked her to try my food and she stuck out her tongue like she was sick. I didn't appreciate that so I moved out and lived with a Korean girl. We got along great! She loved my cooking and we had similar cultures. I realize that I was more comfortable being with Asians because they understood me better, although I had many other friends who were Hispanics, African Americans, and Whites. I get along with people of cultures other than the White ones but it's harder for some of them to appreciate my culture and differences. There are few who want to be my friends and learn about my culture. I see that people relate to their own cultures better. I see that our campus is very diverse but segregated. I don't see a lot of interactions with other cultures. I would love to see that happen on our campus.

THE BLACK GIRLS SPAT ON US

Growing up in suburbia, before busing was started, I did not attend school with any Black children. There was one incident that occurred when I was in elementary school (I don't remember what year) in which they sent us home early because the Black Panthers were in Inner City marching toward Affluent City and I remember everyone seemed afraid. There are two other incidents that stick out in my mind. The first one occurred in a rural high school I attended for one year. I was preparing for my next class after gym and I was standing in the girls' room in front of one of the mirrors combing my hair. A Black girl much larger than me shoved me and said, "Quit combing that red shit on me." Well, I was terrified because I had not realized it but I was the only White girl in the restroom and about five girls started pushing me out of the restroom. I gladly left but I was very afraid. The other occurrence was in high school back in Inner City. I was a member of a pom-pom drill team and we had just performed during the half-time break of a football game. Several Black kids were standing at the end zone and spat on us as we passed by. When we left the game, they threw rocks at our school buses. It was not long after that incident that night football games were rescheduled for day games.

I have not currently had the opportunity to get to know many people at PAYE college of any race or nationality but the former job I had with Airline Company put me in contact with many different types of people from all areas. I attribute that job with giving me the ability to realize that people are people regardless of their color or nationality. I was able to make many friends with Blacks and

Hispanics. We all attended many social functions together and I don't remember any problems due to a person's race or nationality. For many years, and still to this day, my parents have enjoyed the friendship of Black couples and a Greek family. We frequently visit each other's homes.

I honestly do not know for sure if I would marry a person of another race. I believe that personally I could, but I'm not sure if I would be strong enough to withstand the still prominent social attitude against it, and I definitely would not subject my daughter to public ridicule. The stigma is not as bad now as it used to be but it still is not considered "normal."

I DIDN'T UNDERSTAND THE VIOLENCE ALL AROUND ME

My childhood was very interesting in some ways because my parents did not raise me to be prejudiced. My father was in the United States Air Force, which meant that we had to travel a great deal. In some respects, I feel this gave me some advantages over those Black children who never had the opportunity to leave the Black community in which they were raised.

By moving from one place to another, I came into contact with many people with various racial backgrounds. I never felt the impact of racial conflict until Martin Luther King, Jr. was killed. We lived in a mostly Black neighborhood in Inner City, and we had a very nice elderly couple living next door to us. Before the riots broke out after the death of King, we often visited the older White couple. The White lady would make me tons of Barbie doll clothes for my Barbie doll. They were very nice to everyone on the block. During the riots, many White families were threatened and harassed. I remember my mother giving the old White couple a Black cape to hang in front of their house so that they would be overlooked during the riots. The logic to this was that we had heard that if you put something on your house indicating you were Black then you would be safe.

As a young child I did not understand the reason for all of the violence taking place around us. My mother explained that one of our great Black leaders had been killed and this upset the Black community. This created racial tension between Blacks and Whites. At the time my father was overseas in Vietnam, and we were alone without a man in the house. The couple next door survived the riots and moved out of the neighborhood shortly afterward.

I never really felt the impact of prejudice until I was out of high school and I moved to Tennessee to live with my grandmother. I was lucky enough to get a job working for the school district through a government-funded program called CETA. It was set up to help people get on-the-job training for future employment. Tennessee was very different from living in Inner City because I lived in a very small town. It was very obvious that prejudice existed among the people in the small town. Many of my relatives were surprised that I had a job at the school. Most of the Blacks worked in the clothes factories instead of holding office jobs. The position I held as CETA Coordinator was very exciting. Unfortunately the program didn't last long because of lack of funds. The director of the vocational school, who was White, recommended me for a permanent position at the Board of Education as payroll clerk. I was able to train for the position but I did not get the job because I was Black. There had been complaints about a "nigger" doing payroll for the teachers of the small town. I also noticed how unfriendly the White people were in the stores where we shopped. We were watched very closely as if we would steal something. Even though Inner City, where I lived, had its racial problems, it was not as obvious as when I lived in the small city in Tennessee.

Even after some of the unpleasant experiences of my childhood regarding racial conflict, I feel we are all the same in some respect. Skin color is not a choice, it's a given, and we just have to accept the differences that we encounter. I admit that it's very hard to do sometimes but I refuse to let someone else's ignorance cause me to be ashamed of my race and who I am. I feel that we all are prejudiced in some ways, but most of this is brought on by our life experiences with other racial groups.

Being a Black female there are so many stories that I could share but I would have to write a book. Regardless of how we feel about one another, it takes all of us to make the world go around. We need each other to survive. If Blacks only shopped at Black businesses and Whites at White businesses, we would all suffer the consequences.

HE TOLD ME THE TIME

I was raised in the deep southern United States. Thus, I saw discrimination to the right and to the left of me. As a child, I remember the Ku Klux Klan driving by our house in their cars with their funny White outfits on and remember their rallies near our grocery store. I also saw burned crosses on people's lawns from my school bus. I rode a public city bus to town for piano lessons. All Blacks had to sit in the back of the bus or else stand up. I remember peeking back at them and feeling "funny" when an old Black man would stand and sway about when there were open seats in the White section.

I was scared of Blacks and never spoke to one until I was about fourteen years old. I wanted to speak to one so I went up to a Black man on the streets of our town and asked him the time. He told me, and I was amazed. We lived thirteen miles from town, and there were no minorities of any kind in our area. The only one I ever saw was the man who came to dig our septic tank. My mother was the daughter of a southerner and a northerner and she instilled in me that there was something very wrong here. Something ugly was going on. We had "White only" bathrooms and "White only" water fountains in town. My father, who came from southern poor country Whites, didn't like Negroes and in fact called my mother a "nigger lover" from time to time. She soon learned to keep her sentiments to herself (when he was around)! We learned from both these parents. I have one brother (he is twenty-three) who is a redneck minority hater. The rest of us seem to be quite the opposite (there are six of us). Of course we came to Inner City and things were a bit different for the rest of the kids growing up. They were all under fourth grade at the Inner City move. I was twenty years old.

Living in Inner City since I was twenty years old, I noted residents here have their own brand of prejudice and discrimination; it is much more subtle and not as open, but it is still there. In my hometown my aunts were aghast if you had anything to do with "Catholics." Only Protestants were acceptable and even Baptists seemed a bit below us in status (too evangelical)! My father's transfers took us from Inner City to San Francisco and back to Inner City. In San Francisco, my sister dated and subsequently married an Ecuadorian man and her twin brother met and married an Italian girl. On trips back to Tennessee I had relatives who would not even offer up their hand to shake the Ecuadorian's hand when introduced. They would coldly walk away. On that fateful vacation trip at a point in Kentucky, there was a carload of young White men who pointed rifles at our family as we went through the town and followed us out. They had seen the Spanish-looking guy with my sister in a restaurant. He was a medical student and his father was a San Francisco physician. Still, he was not welcome in Kentucky or Tennessee, even among our relatives. We learned our lesson! The San Francisco living experience broadened the mind of our southern White family. My older brother is now married happily to a Puerto Rican, and he knows better than to ever take her home to Tennessee to meet the rest of the family!

I hardly ever go back to Tennessee any more for various reasons. I am also glad we moved, but in so many ways, though, I miss my homeland. I am glad to be different from my relatives back in the South. When I hear them talk I get shocked and feel sorry for them. I know that they were brought up in this way. I love them but they will never know a great percentage of the world. Their minds are closed down and narrow. For this reason, I am glad to have escaped my homeland.

I have had my sister-in-law (Puerto Rican) and her sisters (half-Black and half-Spanish) in my home many times, and they have had me over in theirs. I have had some great times in my home with my Ecuadorian brother-in-law. I never ever saw a minority in any of the southern schools I attended. I think marriage between Blacks and Whites can cause them and their children much grief. This United States does not like it! My brother already has trouble finding a place where his wife and children are not treated poorly. His wife (such a sweet, kind, and wonderful person) had been ill-treated in Little Dixie. At this time, I would not marry and cause myself and kids this trouble, but if I were in love, it would probably be a different story.

SUMMARY

In these stories we have seen how persons of different racial and ethnic backgrounds, as well as persons from different socioeconomic groups, have been affected by their interaction with other races and ethnic groups and the bitter lessons that they learned from such interactions. These lessons, though sometimes shocking at first, may have influenced the choices made by these people in their later lives. Some have gone on to change their views about "the other race," mostly for the better, upon closer interaction with them.

We leave these essays with the feeling that racism and prejudicial attitudes are embedded in the institutional structure of the country—both formal (school, the workplace) and informal (family, neighborhood organization, peer group) institutions. The family as a social institution is often credited with influencing people's values and in crafting perceptions about the world around them. The extent to which this core institution molds people's attitudes regarding persons of a different race or ethnic background is the subject of the next chapter.

3

Family Matters

This chapter devotes attention to the important roles that home, parents, and community play in indoctrinating children with various, sometimes conflicting, ideologies about people of different racial and ethnic backgrounds. The essayists point to the methods used to pass to children not only xenophilic prescriptions and proscriptions, but also xenophobic stereotypes and prejudices, usually based on the teachings that parents inherited from their own families and other reference groups. The intended objective of these teachings is based on the doctrine of conservation of social energy, which adults feel obligated to execute in the name of preserving their heritage as they know it from one generation to another.

In these essays we see three ways that parents convey their attitudes about people of different ethnic and racial backgrounds. One is through direct and explicit communication of racial, ethnic, or religious attitudes to their children in much the same way they instruct them in all other modes of proper conduct. The second way is by directly controlling the opportunities that children have for interacting with those of other racial and ethnic backgrounds. The third method is through parental engagement in child-rearing practices that directly shape the patterns of "self-regarding" and "other-regarding" attitudes that children develop as well as by establishing a homogeneous socioeconomic, spiritual, and residential lifestyle in which selection of activities and friends comes to be learned and accepted by children. This lifestyle usually excludes individuals and groups who significantly differ in race or religion from the family of the child.

These explicit and manifest aims of parental instruction are underlined by subliminal messages, contradictions, and equivocations that constitute a hidden curriculum from which many children take their diverse attitudes. In many cases, didactic lectures and pep talks about the oneness of the human race and the calls for coexistence are mere lip-service fantasies against prejudice, which are overridden by the actions of parents. Some of the essayists reveal that some parents teach tolerance to children while they (the parents) themselves practice either verbal xenophobia by uttering stereotypes and racial slurs, or active xenophobia, when disparate people move into their neighborhood or wish to mingle with their families. The variety of family backgrounds from which these storytellers come and the diversity of their socialization processes make their stories compelling reading.

MY PARENTS FREAKED OUT

In my opinion, my views on race have changed over the years. I have always thought of myself as an open-minded person, but looking back, I don't think I always thought with an open mind. Growing up, I was never exposed to that many people of different races. I attended Catholic school until I started college. This may, in fact, have played a very important role in my attitude toward other races. There were not many other people outside of my race in my grade school and high school. In grade school I can remember maybe five or six African Americans and maybe two Asians the entire time I was in this particular grade school (second through eighth grade). In high school, there were more people outside of my race, such as African Americans, Asians, and Latinos, but the better part of the school was White. The school had about five hundred students, and I would say maybe 1% was of another race besides White.

My parents have never really been overly racially prejudiced in front of me, although I do know they harbor certain attitudes and stereotypes about other races. However, I can remember instances growing up where I had friends that were African American and my parents reacted differently toward them than they did my White friends. In sixth grade I had a very close friend, who was African American. She was the only one in my class so of course she stuck out like a sore thumb. She was constantly teased and hassled by the other students. I think the others saw her to be different not only because of her color but because of her culture. She talked differently, she acted differently, and the other kids didn't know how to react to this. I was always defending her and always stood by her side. To me she was not "Black" or "different," she was my friend.

I always wanted to have her over to play or when I had slumber parties, but my parents would never let me. They never really said why, but thinking back, I don't think they trusted her because she was Black. They bought into the stereotype that she would damage our house because she was Black and Black people are violent. My grandparents had a pool, and I always had friends over to swim but never Valerie. My grandparents are prejudiced and have said things in front of me like the "n" word, and that Blacks are lazy and violent.

My friends used and continue to use racial slurs. I live in Rural County and to me this county is VERY racist. The White people who live here, I think, feel Black people are trying to, in a sense, take over the country and they just can't stand it. My neighborhood is upper middle class and every time a Black family moves in, three White families move out. My dad has said on several occasions that he can't stand it when the Blacks drive around our neighborhood looking at houses and that when they want to buy one, they get the price down so low just because they are

Black. I guess it is okay for a White family to do this because they work hard and deserve a price break, but the Black community doesn't. I can remember my family driving around this neighborhood before buying a house. Do you think anybody thought twice about it? I doubt it!

My mom has mixed views on the subject. I think she uses the statement, "Well, that was how I was brought up, so I don't know any better way to think," as her explanation for why she is the way she is. To me, this is a crutch. She just doesn't allow herself to see any other views. I think she has some racial views though. She owns her own jewelry store and has been robbed several times, mostly by Black people. I think she feels Black people, as a whole, have taken something from her. I can understand this, but it is still closed minded to think that an entire race of people have committed this crime.

This is not my first semester of college. In fact, this is the fourth college I have been to. I think the most diverse place I have been so far was Kansas State. Manhattan alone has many races living together besides the college population. There are Whites, Blacks, Asians, Iranians, Mexicans, and I am sure a few more that I am not even aware of. This was really the place where I was introduced to people of other races. Besides the obvious, seeing other races on campus, I had the opportunity to make many good friendships with people who are Black. Most of my friends in Manhattan were and are Black. However, I really haven't been friends with too many Black girls. My parents are not too happy about this because the girls I made friends with mostly date Black guys. My parents were and still are afraid that this would rub off on me.

In Manhattan, there were many times I had my Black friends over for parties and get-togethers. They were always welcome. They weren't my "Black" friends, but my friends. They were part of my social and support group. However, here in Inner City, I can't think of too many times when I had someone of another race in my house. I can remember once when my younger sister had some of her friends in high school over and a couple of guys in her class heard about her get-together and dropped by (of course, they happened to be Black). Her friends already at the party were White. My parents freaked out. They wanted my sister to ask these two guys to leave, based on their skin color. It was like they thought there would be trouble (fighting, our house being robbed) if they were there. I think my sister did end up asking them to leave but gave a false reason as to why they had to go.

If you haven't already figured it out, yes, I have dated men outside of my race and, yes, I would marry one. I never used to think I would date someone outside my race because there are so many pressures on you when you do decide to take that on. My friends here in Inner City are fairly tolerant of other races, but they often do make racial remarks and so I wasn't sure how they would treat me. Also, before going to K-State, I had started thinking about dating Black men but was simply too afraid— afraid of what my parents might do (disown me), what my friends would say, and how society around me would treat me.

Well, I am here to say that I have crossed the color line and am proud of it. I couldn't believe the number of mixed couples when I lived in Manhattan (I lived there for four years). It astounded me. Sure, I would see one every once in a while here in Inner City, but everywhere you go there are mixed couples. This made it easier for me to cross the color line as was the fact that most of the friends I made were also dating Black guys. My parents, however, are not really sure if I have dated a Black guy. Yes, I know. How can I say I am proud to have done this when I can't even come out of the closet, so to speak? Well, I think they know but choose not to accept it. I wasn't sure what would happen when I moved back to Inner City—if I met a Black guy that I was interested in, what would I do? Well, I decided that I just can't turn off my attraction for Black men. Don't get me wrong, I am just as interested in White men. If it happens then it happens, and my parents will have to accept it.

On a final note, I will say that I have experienced some prejudice against me for dating Black guys. White guys and even Latino guys will refer to me and the other White girls who date Black men as "mudsharks." Also, when in public with a Black guy you would not believe the stares you receive from other people. I never thought it was such a big deal until I experienced it. I have also received some prejudice from Black women who think all White women are after their men. In bars I have gone to where the crowd is mixed, many Black women will stare you down and make derogatory remarks about you if you are with a Black man. Finally, I have also experienced prejudice from White men I have dated who have found out that I have dated a Black man. They seem to act as if I am now tainted and marked for life. One White boyfriend of mine, who happened to be good friends with mostly Black people, was put off by the fact that I had dated Black men.

It seems sad to me that we are approaching a new century and this is still an issue. I don't understand why we can't get past this. What are we so afraid of? To me that is what racism is—ignorance and fear. Ignorant of the ideas and behaviors of another culture, we fear that we might begin to like and act like those cultures that we seem to deem as bad. If we rid our minds of what we've been taught and throw away our "crutches" and see people as PEOPLE, then we could have a chance at resolving the race problem we have.

MY FAMILY NO LONGER VISITS

South Miami, Florida, is a city that contains a large mixture of different races. There are Cubans, Jamaicans, Mexicans, Blacks, Caucasians, Native Americans, and many others. Though living in a city full of great ethnic culture, my family was completely secluded and kept away from anyone different from us. I went to a very small private school, socialized with their families, attended church with the same people, and grew up never personally knowing anyone who was different from me.

When I became a teenager, a Jamaican doctor and his family bought a house across the street from our home. I was thrilled when I learned that they had two girls my age. However, my father was horrified. He screamed about the neighborhood becoming full of a bunch of "niggers and wetbacks." I knew what he meant since he had expressed this opinion previously, but now these were real people. Caroline and Lisa quickly became my friends, yet I found myself forbidden to speak to them. My father said I should be polite, but keep my distance. His word was the law, but secretly I broke the rules. These were now my friends, and his ignorance hurt me.

Religion was not discussed in our home very often. According to my father anyone who was not a Baptist was a heathen. Funny thing was that he never went to church, unless you count Easter and Christmas programs. Yet, we were forced to attend, so we faithfully rode the church bus. I often thought to myself that the real God must go to another church because surely He was not at ours.

At the age of fifteen, I moved out of my parents' home. This is when I began to meet many different people. I remember being afraid at first, but I soon found out that people are all the same. We all laugh, cry, and feel. I remained in close contact with Caroline and her sister for many years. Whenever I went to my parents' home, my dad was sure to tell me how he had helped some poor, disadvantaged, old, Black person. Somehow he felt this made him appear higher in my eyes. Instead, I felt sorry for someone who hated so much and knew little about love. He was involved in a White extremist group and when a wealthy Black family tried to enroll in the private school that my sisters were still attending, he headed up the protest group to ban them from being admitted. He was protecting my sisters from being brainwashed. I never exactly understood what this meant, but I also did not care. I simply learned that there were certain subjects that were best left alone.

When I was married a few years later, my father went ballistic. He expected me to be married at a prestigious Baptist church, one that would reflect his social standing. Instead, his oldest daughter was being married at a nondenominational (Pentecostal) church. Worse yet, the church was located in the inner city, and there were all sorts of "unmentionable" people that would attend. To my father, the most abrasive idea was asking Alfonso to sing during Communion; how dare I, since he was Black. It was one thing to be pleasant to "niggers," but you do not have to be friends with them. How could I bring such disgrace upon the family? Didn't I know what people would say? Maybe I just did not care about how it would appear.

I did care, but not in the way that was acceptable to them. Somehow my father was able to control his mouth for one evening (thanks to my mother) and I had a church full of people I loved and I knew loved me. Alfonso sang powerfully, and even my father commented on his voice. He said, "Music is about the only thing God gave to these unfortunates," as he toasted my husband and me.

Over the years I have had many different types of friends. I have had Mormon friends, Catholic friends, Muslim friends, and a few atheist friends. I have debated politics, religion, and personal convictions with all of my friends, yet we remain as friends. I have wealthy friends, poor friends, White, Black, educated, and uneducated friends. My relationships are with short, tall, thin, fat, young, and old people. They are all people with something to offer. My family no longer comes to visit and hardly calls, but I don't feel that I am missing out on anything. I am raising my children to trust in people no matter how different they seem. My home is constantly filled with the noise of many races. Should my children choose to date or marry someone of another race, it would not matter. I want them to find happiness in their lives. I tell my children, "Red and yellow, Black and White, they are precious in His sight." So much wisdom is wrapped up in this simple nursery song. If we could just all learn the principles and apply them, the world would be a better place.

THE MORTAL SIN

When I was a child, I moved around a lot. My dad is in the oil business, and we got transferred to a new place almost annually for the first six years of my life so I never really wanted to make many friends. I was afraid to get close to anyone because I knew I would have to leave them soon. But we did finally find a place that we stayed in for seven years—Russell, Kansas. In this town, I don't remember there being anyone of another race except for one doctor. He was a Chinese man who did not speak English very well, but I didn't look at him differently. In fact, I owe him a lot because he saved my little toe from amputation after I stepped on a broken brick, and he saved my brother's foot from amputation after my brother stepped on a rusted nail and did not tell anyone about it, until the infection was so bad that we could smell it. Yuck!!

Even though Russell is a very small town, I never went very far from my house. My best friend lived down the block, and we always played at her house or mine. A couple of times I went to church with her after begging my parents to let me do so. I did not, at the time, know why I had to beg my parents for permission to go to church with her, but now that I look back on it I understand. My family went to a tiny Episcopal church and my friend went to a Catholic church. I didn't know the difference except that her church was so much bigger and prettier than mine and I wanted to go and take a look at it. My parents never told me why they didn't want me to go to her church, but I think, now that I know the differences in the beliefs of the two churches, that they were afraid that I might get confused.

After we moved from Russell when I was ready to start the sixth grade, we went to another small town that is ten miles north of Wichita. While I was there, I came to see that my family, and my father more than anyone, was racist. They had never told me not to like people because of their skin color so I got along with everyone. I honestly did not see any difference in my friends because some of them looked different from me. I remember that sometimes we would go driving around Wichita after dinner and my dad would take us "to see how the poor people lived." I hated him so much for doing that because he didn't even try to understand their situations or realize that it was people like himself who might have caused them to live like that. I remember that he would be so surprised when we saw a White family living "down there with all of the spicks and niggers." I went round and round with him about this until I just accepted that he had his own way and I had mine and we would never agree on the subject.

Ever since I was in high school and began to date guys, my parents always told me that I had better not bring home a Black man. It was the mortal sin in my parents' house, and I didn't dare go against them. Besides that, I went to a high school that had a total of five or six African American students and one of them was a very good friend of mine. My parents never said it out loud, but I knew that they were nervous that I might want to date him someday, but we didn't see each other that way. It was by pure chance and lack of an alternative that I only dated White guys in high school.

That is until I moved to Affluent County. I was only here about a month when I saw the man that I wanted to marry someday. I didn't even get to meet him until two weeks after I had seen him, but I was most certainly infatuated. I didn't know what nationality he was, but I did know that he wasn't White and I did not care. When we finally did meet, it was wonderful and so was he. I found out through chitchat that he was Indian and that his parents had moved here from India after their arranged marriage. That night we had our first kiss after spending what seemed like forever at this party, and I knew I was hooked.

A month after we had been seeing each other I asked him if he would go to Wichita with me to go to my brother's wedding and he said he would. Little did we know that that would be the beginning of a lot of problems. I was so excited to introduce him to my parents without even thinking that there would be a problem. When I look at him I see love and nothing more. Often times I have to remind myself that I am in an "interracial relationship." But, even though he didn't say it up front, that was exactly how my dad saw it. In fact, his comment to my mother (since we don't talk about race issues to each other anymore) was, "What's next? A nigger?" I was so hurt when she told me that, but I didn't care what he thought. I was in love.

The next problem that we faced was his mother. She is so very closed minded when it comes to White people that it is almost pathetic. I understand that she wants him to keep his culture, and I would never try to change that, but this woman has never even met me—and we've been together for over three years. We often talk about what will happen when we get married, and he always says that if she doesn't accept it, that is her problem. I just wish and pray all of the time that she would give me a chance because I know that she could like me and realize that I am good for her firstborn. But that remains to be seen in the future, I guess.

Finally after three years of being with him and realizing that he is not going away, my dad has accepted him. It was very hard for him to do so but my mom, who adores him, laid it all out for my father. She told him that either he opened up and saw my boyfriend for the person he is or perhaps lose his daughter for the rest of his life. Obviously he couldn't allow that since I am his only daughter, so he opened up. Now, everything is great on my side of the family. In fact, my dad and my boyfriend have found things that they have in common and spend hours talking when we go to visit. By the way, my dad now actually invites my boyfriend to come home with me!! Yea!!

After living in Affluent County for three years, I have found friends of all different ethnic backgrounds. I have friends who are African American, Asian, Indian, Hispanic, Greek, and plenty more I'm sure. I have learned a lot from my boyfriend and my dad, as well. My boyfriend taught me to love and accept everyone no matter what. My dad showed me that racism is a learned trait that can, over time, be diminished.

I ALWAYS KEPT MY STAND

The first experience I had with a person of a different race was my first-grade teacher. I was a rowdy little kid, constantly talking and getting into trouble. The technique she had for punishing me was to seat me in one of those single desks where the side comes up so you can't see anyone. While I sat in that desk she made me draw little green men; she thought that by doing that, all of my energy and aggression would come out (yeah, right). I did not like that teacher at all. It was not because she was not of my race, it was just the way she dealt with my behavior. I do not remember even questioning her different color. My teacher lived just down the street from me, and one day while my family and our neighbors were outside, she walked over to discuss my unruly behavior with my parents. We had an Airedale dog, a very passive dog, but when she came over, he grabbed a piece of her pant leg and tore it. My dog did not bite her, he tore her pants. Obviously, she got upset and left. My neighbor then made a remark that it must have been her color that made my dog attack her. However, while the whole incident was occurring I was thinking that my dog did it because he could sense I did not like her and he was protecting me. That was the first time I ever dealt with someone who was racist. I do not recall ever, ever having a thought that she was "different" from me. I truly believe that racism is a learned behavior.

The next time I dealt with racist behavior was when I was in sixth grade. There was a girl who was of a different race in our school; my middle school was primarily White. Everyone was attracted to her, not because of her physical features, but because she was of a different race. Everyone wanted to be her friend. I suppose that would be a bit biased too. Not everyone genuinely wanted to be her friend because of her personality, but because she was not the same color that the rest of us were. I also became her friend and did actually like her for who she was. One time she came over to my house to play, and my grandmother and her boyfriend were there. Thankfully, he waited until she left to make his racist comments about her or I would have been doubly embarrassed. This made me very angry. I politely told him she was my friend and that I did not see color. We got into a big discussion regarding race. I remember my parents never interceded or told me to be quiet, they let me speak my mind. After my grandmother and her boyfriend left, my parents remarked how proud of me they were that I stood my ground, but did it politely.

When I was a sophomore in high school my mother remarried. My stepfather had two adopted sons. Jerry is Vietnamese and Nee is African American. These two were my "new" brothers. We never had an issue regarding race. We did, however, have problems regarding relating to new individuals in all of our lives. Nee and I fought a lot when they first moved in with us, but it was never a racial issue, it just had to do with his taking my clothes without permission and other various sibling rivalries— normal fights brothers and sisters get into. I do remember Jerry going to middle school, and one day coming home crying from school because kids were calling him a "gook." Jerry always seemed to be the one who was slammed for his different race. Nee never really had any issues regarding his race. I wonder if that had to do with his assertiveness. Jerry is more passive, whereas Nee is assertive. Perhaps, people could sense that Nee would not take racist comments without a fight. Unfortunately, Jerry would not say a word to defend himself. It is years later now and neither of them have had to deal with racist people, at least not that I have heard. Even Jerry is now comfortable with his race.

The latest issue I had to deal with regarding someone of a different race was at the agency I work at. I work with people who have developmental disabilities. One Saturday, I took one of my clients grocery shopping. While standing in the checkout line, she pointed to a person of a different race, and said loudly, "They are taking all of our jobs." I quickly told her to keep her comments to herself and that when we get out to the car we will have a discussion about her inappropriate behavior. Once in the car I told her that people, no matter what race they are, are all equal. If her opinions stray from that belief, she is to keep her thoughts in her mind and never speak them. She has a right to her opinion (no matter how wrong I think it is) but it is not appropriate behavior to share it in public. We discussed that many people come to America because it is the land of the "free," and they are just as welcome here as she is. That is when she told me she learned this from her mother. The discussion lasted a very long time. She got angry with me, but I kept my stand. I saw the same client the next day. She told me that she went to dinner the previous night (after our discussion) and was waited on by a person of a different race. She then commented, "Well, I guess everyone needs a job." What a switch from the grocery store. I felt good in what I had done. However, I am not so naive to believe that an instance like the grocery store will not happen again. This is fine with me because I know I will be glad to have the same discussion with her over and over again.

I believe ethnocentrism is the root of many of our racial problems in America. People tend to believe their culture is superior, without even learning of other people's culture. This could also be called ignorance. The issue I had with my grandmother's boyfriend, I believe, relates to the fact that in his "day" people of a different race were not seen as equals, and as the times changed and equality became more prevalent, he did not change. His eyes were still back in the day when he saw himself as superior. Also, as I have stated before, I strongly believe this behavior is learned. If you were to take two infants of different races and raise them together without any reference points of racism, I am confident neither would see each other as better than the other in regard to race. This type of information, or slander, has to come from somewhere. More often than not if a child is racist, you could look to the parents and see that they, too, are racists. It is so unfortunate that we have to deal with such ignorant people. Our society seems to thrive on it. For example, everyone seemed to be fixated on the Rodney King verdict and also the O. J. Simpson trial when the racist police officer took the stand. Americans eat up all the controversy that goes along with racism. People of different races have so much to offer those of races unlike theirs. I find it extremely interesting when I hear people talk of their culture and what they do, as opposed to what my typical day would hold.

We have a long way to go to attaining racial harmony. Hopefully, that day will come. However, in the meantime, it is our duty to see all people of a different race, religion, socioeconomic status, or age as equals and to enforce that fact. I think I have had some experience dealing with this issue and will be glad to stand up and voice my opinion.

WE TOURED THE WORLD

I was born in 1963. My town was a relatively "White" community—in fact, I do not recall people of other races living in my town, and if there were, I was not exposed to them in school or in my neighborhood. My father traveled overseas a great deal throughout my life, running various seminars for his company. He was exposed to several people of different ethnic backgrounds and cultures, and he always shared with us what he learned about where he had been. My parents were super about instilling in us respect for the differences in people from other countries.

I was also raised by our church to believe that Catholics were the best Christians. My mother felt differently and shared her story of being disowned for seven years for marrying a Catholic. I believe that as long as you are a Christian, it doesn't matter what man-made church you belong to. I can remember going to some of my friends' churches once in a while, and my parents felt that it would be a good experience for me. I really liked it! I don't recall the schools I attended expressing any particular attitudes toward people of other religions when I was in grade school. We did study the religions of other countries in my later school years. At home and within the community, I remember people being annoyed with the Jehovah's Witnesses. Once in a while I recall hearing some people comment on the Jewish people being stingy with their money and rather pushy for what they want.

From 1971 to 1973 my family moved to Melbourne, Australia, and I quickly learned a lot of their culture and ways of life. I love Australia and its people! On our way back to America my parents thought it would be an excellent education for their five children to go and visit various countries before returning home. My mother taught in Australia and saved her money to help pay for the trip. We went to Singapore, Thailand, Israel, Italy, Greece, Germany, and England. Our family was exposed to several cultures, languages, and foods—Even the poverty areas along the rivers of the "floating markets" in Thailand. What an education!!!

I believe these experiences helped make me more sensitive to other people's differences. I remember when children played a game and wanted to find out who would be "it," they would chant a poem that went like this as they tagged each person's foot:
"Eenie, meanie, minie, moe; Catch a tiger by the toe; If he hollers let him go; Eenie, meanie, minie, moe."

Some children would substitute the word "nigger" for "tiger" and that bothered me very much. I'm not so sure the children fully understood what they were saying, but I think they knew it wasn't a good thing to say.

My parents had, and have, several friends of different ethnic backgrounds and have had them over to the house for dinner parties. Many times friends we have made overseas have come to stay with us for a while and visit with us. Our neighbors were 100% Hungarian—they spoke with a thick accent and were still fluent in their own language. They used to teach us words in Hungarian, and we had fun learning these words. They used to make us Hungarian goulash, and it tasted delicious.

In college, I had my first African American friends. They lived in the dorms with me. Some of the men asked me out. I remember asking my parents what they thought (sort of as a test), and my dad said, "I don't mind if you date them, just don't marry one." He felt it would cause too many problems in our society, especially with our children.

I feel very fortunate having had the opportunities that I had to be exposed to other ethnic backgrounds and cultures, considering where I was born. I have become more globally aware and more sensitive to people of different ethnic backgrounds and races. I know that I am not free from prejudices, but at least I know I will think twice before I form any opinions on issues regarding race, gender, and religion.

I hope as a teacher I can educate my students and incorporate an effective multicultural curriculum and integrate it into all aspects of school. Last year we had an International Festival as a culminating activity based on our school theme for the whole year—multicultural awareness. It was a complete success, and our staff is looking forward to doing it again next year! We are trying, but we still have a long way to go!

A BLEND OF RACES

Since I attended a magnet school, there was a blending of many different types of ethnic groups. The diversity was so prevalent that none of us thought about it being a "multicultural" school. The foundations of what I learned at that school, which was a continuous progress school, taught me to be proud of whatever level

I was on, and to strive to raise myself to a higher level, if possible. Those years taught me to believe in myself and not let others tell me what to do.

My parents are diverse as well and that probably led to my open views about multiculturalism. My mother is one-half German and one-half Chinese and my father is African American. I realize that their marriage was one that was not very accepted in 1969. However, they did marry and had one child—me. As a result, I am a very unique blending of cultures and hold a great history from each ethnic group. I have never looked at this as something to be ashamed of—I have always accepted that the blending of my race was something unique and something to be very proud of. My father was always afraid that I would be ridiculed or called names when I was a child, and from early on he told me over and over again to stand tall, to be proud, and to never let prejudice or discrimination ever stand in my way. Instead, he always told me to use the pain and anger these things caused and use it to be stronger and rise taller. That is what I still live by today. Though my father passed away when I was a freshman, many of the values he instilled in me remain part of my life today.

My mother, who is a very strong woman, has always raised me to think clearly and to accept people as they are. My parents divorced when I was in second grade, so she raised me alone for many years, while teaching full time. I believe the fact that she is a teacher led me to also want to teach and help others. Since my relatives are Black, Chinese, and German, I believe I have a fairly strong base in understanding multicultural groups. I also have developed a very strong sense of what others think about minorities. Because the blending of my race makes it quite difficult to clearly identify me, it is easy for me to hear the views of non-minority people without them being restrained by my presence. I have learned many things about people and what people believe.

The phrases I most remember as a child were terms such as "honky" or "nigger." I remember calling radios "ghetto blasters" and terms such as that. In some ways, it feels like forever since I heard and spoke in those types of slang.

My stepfather now is English, German, and Scottish. My fiance is Polish and German. My friends are 100% Dutch. My stepbrother is American Indian. I believe that my experiences with people of different races are quite extensive—much more so than other people. For me, being with people of different nationalities doesn't even enter my mind. I guess that's because it's such a part of my life.

As for being willing to date or marry someone of another race, I am getting married to a gentleman who is White, and lived in a very culturally stagnant community until the Hmong arrival. We have talked about how, when he was growing up, there were few people in his neighborhood or school that weren't "White." The community today is very different. However, our relationship is built on much more than the color of skin. For each of us, those differences are what will simply create a beautiful child someday—a perfect blending of both of us. It would be hypocritical to say that I wouldn't marry someone different from my race, because I have three. People are people and all are very special. I only wish that others would realize that, so that they would have the possibility to enjoy the friendship, company, and love of other people.

I WILL NEVER LEAVE ANYONE BEHIND

To say the least, I am grateful for the attitudes that my family has instilled in me regarding accepting those of another race. My father made it clear to me when I was younger that everybody should be treated equally, regardless of their physical or religious differences. I still vividly remember my first lesson he taught me about prejudice. I must have been about six years old and only he and I were on a train cruising through Germany, I believe it was. I recalled my brother mentioning some time before the word "prejudice." Being only six years old I had no clue as to what such a funny sounding word could mean. I took it upon myself to ask the only one who surely could know. My dad looked down at me and told me a frightening story.

"Well, Christopher," he began. "Imagine if you, your mom, your brother Scott, and I all wanted to take a train ride together. And imagine when we got to the train station to get on the train, the people who owned the train would not let Scott come with us."

I didn't understand.

"But why wouldn't he be allowed to come? Did he do something bad?" I inquired.

"He didn't do anything wrong. See you, your mom, and I all have brown hair and hazel eyes. Scott has blonde hair and blue eyes. Since he doesn't look like us, the people would make Scott stay here."

I could not believe it. We would have to leave him behind? That's not right. I love him. I don't care what he looks like.

"That's bad," I replied. "Just because he looks different he couldn't be around us?" I asked.

"That's right. That's what prejudice is. Prejudice is leaving someone out because they're different. I hope you remember how you felt if you had to leave Scott behind."

I'll always remember. I would never leave anyone behind. In fact, two of my best friends are of different races. Dennis has a Caucasian father and Korean mother. We have been best friends since high school and will be for a long time to come. My other friend, A. J., has an African American father and a Japanese mother. He has got to be the funniest person on this earth. I love spending time with him. I can honestly say that I have never, ever, ever thought about leaving these two special people behind. They have been there for some of the worst times of my short life, and I don't know where I would be without them.

I don't believe that school played a major part in influencing my values. It did, however, allow me to socialize with others of different racial and ethnic backgrounds on a daily basis. I was raised on military posts, so you can imagine that I have been around people from all over the world. I have been friends with, or at least acquainted with, Caucasians, African Americans, Asians, Hispanics, a German girl, an English girl, twins from Kuwait, and a kindergarten teacher with Native American roots. I suppose you could say that I grew up in a pretty diverse salad bowl.

Thankfully, I have not experienced much racial tension. One time does stand out, however. This must have been about a year or so ago. Dennis, A. J., and I were casually strolling around the mall, just being bored teenagers wasting a Saturday away. We stumbled upon this drunk guy hanging around this carousel type thing, groping on teenage girls and begging them to get it on with him. A. J. decided to intervene, just being the angel that he is.

"Hey, man," he called. "Why don't you leave those girls alone and go sleep it off."

The drunkard turned and glared at the three of us.

Brace yourself.

"Why don't you mind your own business you stupid f——g n——r!"

My jaw hit the cold tile floor. I could not believe that guy actually said that! Not just said it, he basically screamed it in front of a hundred people! The next thing I knew A. J. was carrying me on his back, streaking up the stairs after this bigot. I was begging him to let it go, that he could get in trouble with the law. You have to know A. J.; he's really strong and he's hot tempered. I was really worried. Luckily for the drunkard, and in a sense for A. J., security caught up to him and threw him out. The point is that I thought these things only happened in movies and on news footage. No. People everywhere think like that drunken bastard. They are the ones who should be left behind.

I attended Pittsburgh State my freshman year of college. I was fortunate enough to live on a floor with a variety of different racial groups. My next door neighbors were African Americans, and they were pretty cool to hang out with. Down the hall was an Asian art major who painted the upstairs lobby. Great guy. Couldn't really understand him though, but he was friendly. Everyone got along with everyone else, except for this one African American student at the end of the hall. I don't think he shared my views about integration. Every time I tried to be friendly and cordial with a warm greeting, he would scowl at me and my friends. I swear I overheard him in the bathroom talking about the "punk-ass White boys" down the hall. I learned rather quickly that you can do anything in your power to love everyone, but you won't necessarily get it in return.

Interracial dating and marriage is something I have no problem whatsoever with. I think if a woman and I are compatible and I am totally infatuated with her, it makes no difference to me if she has blonde hair, brown skin, or a thick accent. Besides we're all the same color when the lights go out, right? I have never dated anyone of a different race, but I have never gone out of my way to avoid any. At the same time, I have never pursued any either. We'll see what happens in the future.

I think that chat my dad and I had fifteen years ago really had a powerful impact on my relationships with people who are different from myself. I have to think how I would be if my dad let them leave Scott behind. Let's not go there. Let's just enjoy the train ride together.

UNIQUE GRAINS OF SAND

We live in a social world. Since birth, most of us have been significantly influenced by our families, friends, teachers, politicians, musicians, and the like. It is out of this complex and diversified framework that many of our initial attitudes and beliefs are influenced and created. Our unique personal morality, which includes our racial and ethnic views, is taught, formed, and challenged early on. Initially, we may not have the cognitive capacity to discern the importance of understanding our family, racial, or ethnic history. Yet, we simply accept its natural existence. And as we come to accept our own heritage, many of us discover a strong identity and sense of belonging. Consequently, because our identity comes from knowing about our heritage, we may thirst for greater knowledge. That is, in a world of many grains of sand, we not only want to find our own unique place on the beach, but we want to come to understand our uniqueness.

My personal cultural paradigm followed much the same acquistional pattern. My earliest childhood memories include traveling to my grandmother's cottage in northern Wisconsin and dancing to Polish songs on the pine-needled gravel way. Initially it was these types of summer gatherings that exposed me to my Polish ancestors' stories. Even today, I continue to enjoy listening to grandmother's stories of surviving as a Polish woman in a predominantly German neighborhood.

My childhood cultural paradigms may thus far seem egocentric. On the surface, my knowledge and pride in my personal heritage may seem to counteract the achievement of a "broadened cultural perspective of all world cultures" that James A. Banks (1991) proposes in his book *Teaching Strategies for Ethnic Studies*. Yet, further revelation of personal examples will demonstrate how many of my childhood experiences have exposed me to other cultures. This exposure and my personal contacts with many culturally diverse people have helped me become more "ethnically literate." In fact, this exposure has helped maintain my familial pride and curiosity.

For example, one of my fondest childhood memories involved bedtime stories. Many of my favorite childhood stories had culturally diverse main characters. Some of these stories included "Free to Be You and Me," "Mary Jane," and "Inspector Pickett." This fact alone surprises me, as during the 1970s there were not as many culturally diverse children's books as there are today. I even recall watching "Sesame Street" in which an African American and a Mexican American were narrators. This was a very subtle and yet positive image that Whites were not the only people on television.

In addition to childhood literature and music, I remember certain key events in which I came in contact with people of different races. One situation involved a time when my cousin married an African American man. I do not remember the specifics of the event as much as I remember the response to one of my curiosities being, "Black is beautiful, White is beautiful." Again, another positive image was given about people who had a different heritage.

Yet there were also childhood experiences and exposures that were not positive images. Arguably, I still feel that even these exposures have helped me become more culturally literate. One of these experiences involved a car ride through an Indian reservation. It was a summer day, and the driver had stated that "we should roll up the windows in the event that the Indians shoot an arrow at us." Actually this comment made me more curious about the American Indians as human beings. Fortunately, I had a chance to turn this derogatory comment into a positive learning experience. Years later, during my collegiate years, I chose to find out more about this culture. I had a wonderful opportunity to tutor several American Indian students in mathematics and English. Indeed, we learned many things (beyond the curriculum) from one another. What happens to children who hear this comment time and time again and are given no opportunity to discover another culture for themselves? Stereotypes are perpetuated unless a person is allowed an opportunity to learn and experience another culture.

Another collegiate cultural experience I had occurred when I was teaching in a predominantly Hmong elementary school. This experience gave me an opportunity to not only work with these students but also to work, learn, and communicate with the students' families in the context of a different culture and language. This experience particularly sensitized me to the importance of learning and understanding my students' heritage in order to better relate to them and address their needs. Frequently it is tempting to teach them what one considers to be the "best" curriculum for them. This single-mindedness ultimately negates the importance one's unique cultural identity has in establishing one's sense of efficacy.

Both the understanding of one's own culture and an exposure to other cultures appear to be an adequate solution to ensure an appropriately tailored student-directed curriculum. Yet an overly simplistic cultural curriculum also has its caution signs. Frequently children are expected to simply memorize facts about other races and ethnic groups. This "skimming the surface" approach does little to encourage higher level thinking and may even aid in maintaining old cultural assumptions.

Although admittedly my own education contained some aspects of this "low level" curriculum, even in my predominantly White community, there were also ample opportunities for cultural exchanges. Personally, I went on a cultural exchange program to France. My cultural literacy continues this summer when I will be teaching in New Zealand. I will be teaching Maori children and living with a host family. Therefore, my own education and current teaching style have been positively affected by the gradual transformation to a more multiculturally sensitive and challenging curriculum.

In addition to my culturally broadened education, I have also had the opportunity to establish ethnically and racially diverse friendships. Truly, I have discovered that it is the heart that matters. Consequently, I would not hesitate to marry someone of a different race.

In conclusion, like most people, I am proud of who I am and where I came from. It is a large part of what makes me unique. It is a large part of what makes every person unique. My personal heritage gives me a sense of belonging. However, we do not live in a seashell. We live on a beach. And it is our human responsibility to learn about the other grains of sand if we are to prevent the vicious tide from washing us out.

MIXED MESSAGES

First, I'll address impressions I inherited regarding racial groups. My father was an Irish Catholic. My mother was a German (from Russia) Protestant. I was taught by both parents, luckily, never to call anybody a racial slur or to look down upon them because of their race. Of course, they were typical people of that generation where "do as I say, and not as I do" was very common. They taught me not to be racially prejudiced, yet I detected their own prejudices in the things they said and did.

Though my parents taught us to never use racial slurs, I did, but not often, hear them use the word "nigger." It seems that the main usage of this term was in the phrase "worked like a nigger." After a particularly grueling day at the grind, one of my parents may use this expression in describing all their hard work. This expression actually could be construed as both good and bad: it may assume that "niggers" are the ones delegated, and only ones deserving, to do the hard work, but it may also be complimenting the amount of hard work "niggers" actually do.

My family was fearful of Blacks (in their day, they were referred to as the "colored" or "Negro" people). There was little mixing of the White and Black races when they grew up. They saw Blacks as a socioeconomic underclass, with such a group's accompanying problems of poverty, poor housing, menial jobs, and high crime. Often times when my parents, and the Whites they knew, did have their few encounters with Blacks, it was while being victims of crime. That, I believe, made the Whites fearful of the Blacks. For example, my maternal grandfather (who died before I was born) was knifed and robbed once by a Black man in the restroom of the Union Station. Also, once while on a date, a Black man came up to the car my mother and her date were sitting in, and knifed her date. These two incidents, of course, left bad feelings in my mother's family. I think because there was so little mixing of the races, and as often times the "mixing" that may have occurred was of such a negative type, this fueled the fire of prejudice. My mother's family really didn't have many experiences of a pleasant variety with Blacks so this made them fearful of Blacks and led them to believe that Blacks, as a group, were violent and dishonest.

Likewise, though, my parents did speak kindly of some Blacks whom they had association with during their lives. After World War II my parents part-owned an appliance store. They had some customers and, I believe, people who work for them who were Black and whom my parents spoke very kindly of, as being very nice people. While operating this store my parents ran into people of all races who had very bad credit problems and didn't pay their bills. I'm sure they had some Blacks who had such bad credit, but the Blacks certainly weren't the only race that had such problems. They may have had a higher percentage of Blacks whom they turned down for credit or who didn't pay their bills, but I can see how the Blacks at that time would have had a much tougher time economically than most groups.

My dad worked at the packing houses for several years as a young man. He described how hard and strenuous this labor was. I remember him saying how, during the depression, there could be one hundred men standing outside the packing house looking for a job every morning, and they would pick maybe three or four of the biggest men to work. He used to say how hard they worked and I remember him mentioning how hard some of the Blacks worked at this job. He was trying to make the point to me of how hard a job this was. I now suppose he implied that since the Black man was working there, it was very hard work indeed.

I went to Catholic schools from kindergarten up through and including high school (twelfth grade). The nuns basically taught us not to be prejudiced. I had no Blacks at my grade school of approximately eight hundred children and about fifteen Blacks may have attended my coed high school of approximately six hundred students. The few Blacks at my high school were accepted and seemed to get along fine. In fact, in the class ahead of me, one Black boy, Sylvester James, was actually a school hero. This is a bit odd, especially as it was in the late 1960s. Sylvester was an outgoing, witty, very popular guy. He also sang and played in a band that entertained at high school dances. A second Black student, Thomas, was a senior class president in 1969 and I believe he was actually the only Black student in his class. Now, in 1991, I run into Thomas in the court system. He is a well-known attorney working for one of the more prestigious law firms in Inner City.

Other institutions, such as television and movies, instilled racial attitudes in me. Blacks were not very visible in the entertainment media. With, of course, some exceptions, Blacks were often portrayed in powerless roles, doing menial jobs. In the 1960s the entertainment industry seemed to give some good eye-opening views of the world through such movies as *Guess Who's Coming to Dinner*, the "All in the Family" television show with Archie Bunker being the butt of the humor, and many other movies and shows portraying Blacks in a better limelight and revealing prejudices as being unfair.

MY PARENTS' DOCTRINE

I was lucky to have two parents who were of different religions. I think this made us all more tolerant of each other and all religious groups. I especially feel this way when I compare my family with some of my friends' families who were traditional, conservative Catholics. When I was ten years old my mother, who had been Evangelical, was baptized Catholic. My dad didn't have to go to church by himself then, so it worked out just as well. My mother's change of religion showed me a tolerant attitude toward religion. She never attended her church regularly, anyway, so that taught me a liberal view toward religion. She taught me that how one lived and treated other people was more important than one's religious beliefs. I believe this was a nice attitude she instilled in me.

I think I was lucky that of my father's five Catholic siblings, not one of them married a Catholic—which was unusual for Catholics back in the 1930s and 1940s. Having such a mixture of relatives was nice in that nobody was taught only one view of things from a religious standpoint. I was supposed to like all my relatives and I did, so I knew their religions couldn't be so bad.

The Catholic schools taught us that Catholics were superior, of course, but the 1960s helped most of us Catholics see that for what it was and discard most of the religious training we got. The Catholic schools taught us the old Baltimore Catechism, which is quite conservative Catholicism. We knew we were the one, true religion and we just kind of pitied everybody else because we thought they were so off track and not as fortunate as we. I remember proudly buying pagan babies in the missions as a child in an effort to save their souls and to enable them to be Catholic. My religion certainly taught provincialism and superiority.

As an adult, I accept the responsibility that I can think things out on my own. I realize that I was taught many wrong, incorrect things in the Catholic schools, yet I don't regret the fact that I attended them, for I gained discipline and other attributes that outweighed the wrong things about my Catholic education.

I started college in 1970 so I have had plenty of opportunity to know many different types of people. Attending college from 1970 to 1974 allowed me to meet new people, but not really people who differed greatly from friends in my previous schooling. I lived at home during college. It was a commuter college, and because I attended school and worked at the same time, I did not really have time to get to know different people like going away to a college and living in a dorm would have allowed.

After I graduated from college, I lived and taught school in Sydney, Australia, for almost two years. That experience really opened up my view of the world. I traveled quite a bit during that time to places such as New Guinea, New Zealand, Fiji, and Mexico. I have had the urge to travel ever since and feel that traveling can truly be an education in itself. I don't mean the "lay on the beach" kind of traveling, but rather the "ride the local transportation and talk to the local people" type of traveling.

The different careers I've had allowed me to work with a variety of people. For the last ten years I have worked in a legal setting among many attorneys and also with many Blacks, since state and county government jobs especially seem to hire many Blacks. I have grown through the years in my understanding of the world and its peoples, and would like to see a world where there are no racial, socioeconomic, religious, or cultural divisions and categorizations. I think we are arriving at a time, especially in the United States, where we need to respect all people as being fellow humans and stress our commonalities and disregard ethnic and racial distinctions. Since none of us chose who our parents were or their race and creed or what they did in their lives, I don't think we should have to live our lives mainly in their legacy.

In the United States, as Jessie Jackson puts it, rather than a melting pot, we are more like a fruit salad. That may be true. But I would like us to grow beyond our ethnic and social identities. As we are now living in a global village, we need to identify as equal humans with racial and ethnic differences that are not as important as our oneness in inhabiting this planet together. We need to live harmoniously, in mutual respect, because although we are all different, we are really all the same.

From my American legacy, I suppose I believe in individualism and the importance of the individual. We need to respect each other as individuals and judge each other on our own merits and not by standards that we had no choice about, such as our race or ethnic group. If we can achieve this mutual respect, then maybe we can all work for our common good and perhaps then we can identify ourselves as equal members of one global village.

MAYBE I SHOULD BE A PARENT FOR A WHILE

I grew up in a small town and in a wealthy family. We were taught to be well-mannered and weren't to speak until we were spoken to. My brothers, sister, and I couldn't get any grades below a C or we were grounded with absolutely no privileges until the next report card came out. We weren't to run around with poor children or children who were criminals. Our friends had to match our family exactly. We couldn't even run with Blacks. There weren't people of other nationalities in my small town, so nothing was ever said about that. I hated it!

I didn't have a chance to run around with anyone Black because there weren't many in our town. I did have a babysitter once who was a Jehovah's Witness. She taught me a lot about morals, about dressing right, not too sleazy. She told me not to chase men and taught me how to be a better person. When I gave her a Christmas present, though, she wouldn't accept it.

As far as school goes, I always got away with murder because of my parents' status. I used to skip school and smoke in the bathrooms, and I always got in fistfights with my older brother. When we were at school, we went crazy because the school wasn't as strict as our parents.

I was exposed to drugs and alcohol in school, even stealing. I did engage in social drinking. In high school, the word "nigger" was used; my parents used it also. My parents said Blacks were poor and would steal. They wouldn't even let me associate with boys because they were afraid I would get pregnant. They were also strict on my brother about running around with girls. They never liked my boyfriends or my brother's girlfriends.

I moved to Inner City right out of high school. I have supported myself for seven years and started college a year ago. As soon as I got away from my parents, I realized that poor people, regardless of their race, are people too! Just because they are different and aren't as fortunate as me doesn't make them bad people.

I have worked with people of other nationalities. Sometimes we didn't understand each other because our languages were different, but we managed to get along and relate by using our hands and sign language. My roommate is Mexican American. The nationality difference isn't a problem with us. Right now, I am dating a man who is half Japanese and half Indian. I am American and Italian. The nationality difference isn't a problem with us either. It's what is inside a person that really matters; not where he came from. Besides, he is very good looking. He is Baptist, and I've never been baptized. It's not that I don't believe in God, but my parents never baptized me and I just don't know what religion to commit to. We have the same moral attitudes about almost everything so we get along well.

As soon as I broke away from my parents, I could speak to whomever I wanted and I was able to have friends of different nationalities and origins. People are people no matter where they come from or what color they are. There are always going to be bad people in every race and in different parts of the world. You just can't say that all Blacks are bad and all Whites are good. I know because I've been exposed to a lot of different kinds of people. I know a man who went to prison for dealing drugs and who happens to be White. Since he has been out of prison, he hasn't engaged in those activities anymore. Although he was a prisoner, he is a good person and has a heart of gold.

I am also bothered by materialism. My family based everything on material things. If we did something good, we would get a present of some sort. I maintained good grades my first two years in high school so my dad bought me a brand new car for my sixteenth birthday. But my family also took material things away if we did something bad. I got a D in biology in the eleventh grade, and my dad took my car away and sold it.

Status was also very important to my parents since they both are rich, career people. They get upset because I used to be a waitress. They would say only dirty, poor people worked as waitresses. I worked in a bar for a while as a cocktail waitress, but I didn't dare tell them because they probably would have disowned me from the family.

Now I am working at the United States Department of Education, Office of Secretary's Regional Representatives. My parents are very happy since I have an important "desk job." I didn't do it for them though. I just happened to get lucky and found out about the job, and I got it. It's so nice to get a job because of myself and my skills and not because I'm Dr. Cummings's daughter. That's how it was back home. I could get a job anywhere I wanted because of my parents. It is so nice to be myself and not what my parents wanted me to be.

Last Christmas I took my roommate home with me because she and her daughter were going to spend Christmas alone. My mother took me in another room when we got home and scolded me for being with her. My roommate is very overweight and very unattractive. But what my mother didn't take the chance to find out is that she has a heart of gold and is the best friend a person could have. I scolded my mother back and told her that even though she was a fifty-five-year-old woman and had accomplished a lot, she still had a lot to learn about life and people.   My mother did give my friend a chance and now likes her.

Now I am twenty-five and I speak my mind to my parents. We fight a lot but we are getting closer. I've taught them a lot. Inner City is totally different from the town in which I grew up. Maybe I should be the parent for a while!

LOYAL TO MY FAMILY

Before I began school, I never had any contact with the outside world except weekly trips to the grocery store. I lived in Affluent County until I was a freshman in high school, and I sincerely doubt that any people who were noticeably of a different race shopped at our grocery store. I started kindergarten at Oak Grove Baptist School in August of 1977. Every student there was White, and we were obviously of the same religion. Even at church on Sunday, there were only White people.   We were, however, taught a song called "Jesus Loves the Little Children"—Red, Yellow, Black, and White. We saw pictures of these people, yet we never came face to face with them. We were taught to love all people, not just White people. I stayed at this school until I was out of the seventh grade.

My grandfather has quite a bit of Indian blood in him and is very proud of it. I speak of my mother's father. He is very much a farmer—built his own barn and greenhouse. He grows many herbs, plants, fruits, and vegetables. He does not celebrate "Thanksgiving" because he mourns for his people who were tricked, cheated, and killed.

My father is prejudiced. I'm not sure if he is against all races but White, but I know he is prejudiced against Black people. He calls them "dumb niggers."

Back to school. I entered eighth grade and had my first exposure to people of different religions and races. The people of different races hung out together with people of their own race. I basically did not notice them. The exceptions to this were one mean Mexican boy who tormented me daily and a group of three loud Black boys who never spoke to me. I became very curious about those who were of a different religion. I had never before met anyone who believed in a different God, a different interpretation of my God, or in no God at all. I mostly met Catholics and atheists. When I started asking questions, I found that half of my family on my father's side is Catholic. It did not make sense to me that other people did not know and love my God as I did. I thought those kind of people lived in jungles in foreign worlds. I spent quite a bit of my eighth-grade year talking about God with my parents.

I started high school at Shawnee Mission North. However, I was only there for one semester. I stayed close to my best friend Teresa and didn't notice much else. I switched high schools because I moved to Missouri to live with my father. I didn't know any people of other races, but the students I did know spoke very lowly of them. I think I hated Oak Park High School for just that reason. The Black students sat in the very back rows of the bus and the classrooms.

When school got out, I moved again. I started my sophomore year at Park Hill High School. Here I made my first Black friend. Her name is Camille Allen, and she is one of the sweetest people I have ever met. I never thought any differently about her than I did about any of my White friends. The summer of my junior year, I went to Pensacola with my boyfriend to visit his father. One night we were walking down a side street from a bar to our car when my boyfriend's father began to tell us how the Black people lived in Florida. He said that the Black people drove big old cars and would back out in front of White people so that the White people would rear-end them. Then they would live off the insurance money they collected. I laughed at this because it seemed clearly to be verbalized prejudice. Within ten minutes of Mr. Barnes telling us this, a car full of Black people backed out in front of us and stopped. Mr. Barnes did not hit them, however, because he was prepared.

My first semester after I graduated from high school, I went to Maple Woods Community College. I became good friends with a Black gentleman. I moved to the Plaza in January of 1991. I began attending Inner City Community College and working at a 7-11 on Main Street. At school, I began a friendship with a Japanese girl. At work, I became friends with a half-Black and half-White guy. The assistant manager of the store is from Pakistan.

I have forgotten to mention my house guest for August of 1990. He was a student from France, assigned to my family from LEC. I looked forward to his arrival but grew to dislike him greatly. I found him to be very egocentric. He constantly spoke of the superiority of France, pointing out every fault he could find in Inner City.

I do not think that I would date a man of a different race, let alone consider marrying one. But I do not think of it as prejudice. I know that my family could not, would not, accept him. I know that would hurt him as much as me.

I have written this paper from the point of view that I see Blacks and Whites as equal in my eyes. However, when I am at work, some Black men will make crude sexual remarks to me. This has caused me to feel some fear when some of them come in. That's the only difference.

NEVER TRUST THEM

We have all been socialized since early childhood and continue to be socialized by people, television, news, and situations. This socialization develops our biased thinking. We develop prejudices and stereotypes about things or people who are different from ourselves. Not all prejudices and stereotypes are bad, but the majority of the ones that are prevalent are not good. The good prejudices and stereotypes help us to better understand and interact with others. The bad prejudices and stereotypes create myths or assumptions about others that are not necessarily true.

Since I came from a Christian family, my parents taught me to love everyone and not to judge people. Growing up I saw bias toward people of my ethnic background. In school, we were taught a White perspective of American history, but when I got home, I received the entire story, not just one side. I was taught never to trust the White people. You can be friends with them but should never become intimately close with one. I believe the reason for this is because of our past dealings with the White man. And rightfully so, you learn from the past, and it should not be forgotten, although it should remain in the past.

The Christian faith was number one in our household. We attended church every Sunday, morning and evening. We went to Wednesday night services and were active in our church. Not only were we active in our church but the Bible was studied in our home and put to practice. I was taught the Christian faith, but it was not forced upon me. The faith was presented to me and it was my choice to accept it or reject it. This doctrine is even a part of the Christian faith. It is your choice. Being a Christian doesn't make you any better than anyone else because you are just a sinner who is saved by God's grace. The difference is that you are trying to be more Christ-like.

I attended public school up to the sixth grade. My impression of the public school was good then. The teachers took interest in the students and wanted to teach the students something. My parents, exercising their responsibility, decided to remove me from the public school system, because they saw how rapidly the standard of education was declining. I was enrolled in a different school, because I was going to junior high, and my parents were rich. Therefore, I was enrolled in a private school. Not just any private school; I attended Tri-City Christian High School, where they tried to mold me into a saint.

One negative experience I remember was in grade school. I did well in all of my schoolwork and was placed into an accelerated class. In this special class there were only Whites in the class, except me. The students wondered what I was doing in the class. They had been socialized to believe that people of color were less intelligent than they. This still happens in other situations. When I walk into a nice, expensive restaurant, all of the Whites take a second glance.

College has opened up the minds of many people, but there are still people who wonder why I am at the university I attend, because it is not typical for a person of color to attend this university.

College was where my thinking was expanded and my personal ideas were freely expressed. In college I met various other "different" types of people. One thing I recognize, however, is that all people like to associate with people who are like them.

Do I have "jungle fever"? I think we are all curious about people who are different from us, and we are afraid of people who are different from us. I would be willing to date someone of a different race. I am not sure about marriage. I believe that marriage is meant for persons who are in love. If that happens then I would change my mind.

MY PARENTS BLEW A GASKET

When I look back on my childhood socialization and my impressions and attitudes toward different races and religions, I think of my grandparents' home. My dad's parents lived in Milwaukee. I was told that the neighborhood was bad. I remember driving with my family, and as soon as we got off the expressway, I could hear the noise of the doors being locked. My parents and grandparents were very prejudiced against Blacks. All around their house were Black people. I remember noticing that everyone was Black except we and thinking that we were not supposed to be there because of our color. My parents always told us not to talk to anyone and to always stick together. But I realize now, we were never outside. We were always inside their home. My grandfather would walk everywhere because he did not know how to drive. Anyway, one day a Black man came up to him and mugged him. The man hurt my grandfather, and that is when I started believing that Blacks were bad people.

Growing up, the school I went to was a parochial school. There were only White students in the school. Everyone at my school was also Catholic. You could say I did not encounter different religions until high school, and I never really encountered any other race until I entered high school. The high school was an all-girl parochial school. There were different races and religious groups, but not as many as there are in a public high school. In high school, I did not care whether a person was Chinese, African, Jewish, Lutheran, or anything. I saw these classmates of mine as people, and, to tell you the truth, I am surprised at how open minded I was, given the influence of my parents and grandparents. I saw people for who they were, and maybe I learned this from my sisters and brother. They had friends of different races and religious groups, and I feel this helped my parents believe that everyone is the same no matter what. I believe my parents were trying to protect us from any danger when we were young. As we got older my parents started opening up their world.

As the years went on the biggest challenge my parents would ever have to deal with happened. My open-minded sister told my close-minded parents that she was pregnant and the father was a Black man. My parents almost blew a gasket. Well, this certainly was the turning point in my parents' lives. They realized color or sex or anything else does not matter, just what the person is like on the inside. I am so proud of my parents and how far they have come with dealing with their prejudices. Their views have changed.

Today I have a four-year-old nephew who is half White and half Black. I love him so much and I think the world of him. I do not see him as anything but Larry. I see the beautiful eyes and the adorable smile and the sassy way of his. Larry's father is always welcomed into my parents' home. They love Larry and Ben so much, it does not matter that they are Black at all. It should not anyway. Larry is my mother's buddy. They are inseparable because my sister works hard to provide for Larry, so my parents have Larry a lot. My family is prejudiced in one way with Larry. We think he is the cutest boy ever!

It is wonderful to see how far my family has come. We are all so welcoming and willing to help anyone. We accept people for who they are and not what they believe in or look like. We are a very close family, and we all have strong faith. I know our faith brought my parents to open their hearts to the wonderful, diverse world we live in.

It is strange to think that if we did not have Larry, I don't know where we would be at in life. I think my parents would be shallow people. Yes, everyone has prejudices, but people deal with them differently. And not all prejudices are related to race, sex, or religious groups. In society today, you must be willing to accept everyone for whom they are. To tell you the truth, I am very scared for my nephew Larry. The reason I am scared is because of his race. I hope that his schoolmates will see Larry as a person who has feelings and not for the color of his skin. I wonder sometimes where Larry will fit in? Will he say he is White or Black or both, if someone asks him. I hope that children do not exclude him or are not mean to him in any way. Larry is like everyone else, except he has the best of two worlds. My sister did not bring Larry up with just a White background. She has acquainted Larry with his two heritages. I believe my nephew, Larry, is one of the luckiest children around. Not everyone can say they have the best of two worlds.

ALL WELCOME

I grew up in a small rural town of about 3,000 people. There really wasn't anyone different from me in my neighborhood or my church. There was one girl in my school who was from India and another boy, who, I think, was from Latin America, or somewhere near there. Although these two people were a part of our school, I never heard any racial slurs from teachers or students about these people. Maybe people said those kinds of things, but I never heard any of it. In fact I can't remember even hearing derogatory statements toward any race come from my parents, my school, or my church.

As a young child, I was exposed to several different races. When I was probably in about first or second grade, we had a young man from Cuba stay with us for six months to a year. He was a refugee sent over by the government, and he needed a place to stay and someone to sponsor him, so he could stay in the United States. When he moved in with us, he hardly spoke any English, and we only spoke a little Spanish. This made for some funny misunderstandings. He showed us how to make some Cuban food and helped us carve pumpkins at Halloween. Somewhere around that same time my mom taught English to a group of Korean women one night a week and another night she led a Bible study for them. I was never allowed to participate, because I was too young at the time, but we did go to their homes sometimes for social gatherings.

Also, after I was in high school, we became friends with some neighbors of ours, who had adopted two Korean girls. As a young child I had many experiences with people of different races.

I was not exposed to African Americans at all, to my knowledge, until I came to college. I had my first real contact with African Americans, when I went to the south side of Chicago during spring break in 1994. I went to Chicago to learn about racial reconciliation, and I became friends with many African Americans. I really enjoyed it and I went again the next spring. It wasn't until this past summer, though, that I really learned about the culture and background of African Americans. I spent my whole summer in Chicago working with inner-city children and teaching them about Jesus. Several of the other college students who worked with me were African American and I learned a lot about myself, my culture, and how society has instilled prejudices in us. I listened as people shared with me where they were coming from and how things affected them.

Another opportunity I had since coming to college to know people of different races was through Campus Crusade for Christ here on this campus. That is how I met my friend, Ting.

Ting, or Dollar as he likes to be called, is a nineteen-year-old Hmong male. He came over to this country with his parents when he was four or five. His father is a pastor, and that is how his family was able to come to the United States.

I first met Dollar in the spring of my sophomore year. A mutual friend introduced us and then we became friends. We both shared a common interest in singing so we would hang out and sing songs together. As our friendship deepened, I began to ask him questions about the Hmong culture, and he opened up and shared things with me. I was able to put aside the things I had heard from fellow classmates about Hmong people and just got to know Dollar as a friend. I am very grateful for our friendship, and I consider him one of my very close friends.

I have thought a lot about whether I would be willing to date or even marry someone of another race. It has been on my mind increasingly since I spent the summer in Chicago. The answer I have finally come to is that if a person of another race loved me, and I loved him, and we wanted to get married, I wouldn't let the color of his skin stop me from marrying him.

In general I feel that I am very open to people of different races and that I have had a lot of exposure to people of different races. It makes me very sad, though, to know that others don't feel the same way. I am committed to doing what I can to see that racial reconciliation becomes a reality in our lifetime and continues through the end of time. In fact that is what I would like to do when I graduate. I would like to move to Chicago and spend my time telling other people about Jesus and that God wants Blacks, Whites, and every other racial group to be able to live in harmony.

I SEE THE RAINBOW

I can remember far back into my childhood when racial differences were first introduced to me. This came from watching the ever-famous television program "Sesame Street." This show tries to educate children about everyone's differences.

I feel this had a positive effect on my racial outlook. Studies have shown that prejudice is a learned phenomenon and is transmitted from generation to generation through the socialization process. I would have to disagree with this to an extent, because I personally know many families, where the parents are extremely prejudiced, and the children are not. This holds partially true in my family. I have a father, who is one of the most prejudiced people that I have ever met. He has always expressed this to me, ever since I can remember. My mother is in the middle. She used to be pretty racist on some issues, but after working with different ethnic backgrounds, some of her ignorant prejudices have been replaced by reality. However, I feel that she still holds some stereotypical beliefs. I, on the other hand, am a very accepting and open-minded person. I do not hold the color of a person's skin or their religious beliefs against them. I have established this openness from somewhere other than through the socialization of my parents. Although many people do, in fact, actually pick up and carry racist and prejudiced beliefs, I feel that this only holds true in some instances. I feel that my beliefs are a result of personal experiences.

I have been fortunate to have experienced racial and ethnic differences at a very early age. Being from a relatively large city, I lived around all types of people. This was very important in my developing into who I am today and forming certain beliefs. My major experience living with racism and prejudice started when I was in tenth grade and still continues today. You see, I dated an African American very seriously from tenth grade until about a year ago. To some this is not a big deal, but to others it is a "sin." Throughout the four years, I had to deal with racist and ignorant attitudes from people at my high school (teachers and students) and, the hardest of all, from my parents, and stares and evil looks at the mall or wherever we decided to go out.

My parents' beliefs were different from mine as I stated earlier, and the result was that I had to hide this relationship from them. Yes, I hid this from my parents for all four years and still have not told them about it to this day. I kept it from them for fear of how they would react or treat me, and because of the fear that they would literally keep me in the house when I was still in high school. To some this may sound like a stupid thing to do, but honestly it was what I had to do. I heard comments from my father such as "the day you bring home a nigger is the day I'll disown you!" I successfully hid it from my parents through prom, homecoming, you name it. To this day, though, I seem to be labeled as someone who "dates Black guys," which is ridiculous, because I date all races. However, I was not the only one who received all of the problems, so did my ex-boyfriend. His parents were not that accepting of interracial dating either, so they were also not fully aware of the relationship. He also received a lot of dirty looks from people at school, especially from the African American girls. They looked down on him for dating a "White girl" just as I was looked down upon by many for dating a "Black guy." Believe me the story is definitely a good one for a talk show! We could share so many stories that could be very educating. I learned a lot from this relationship. I learned that there are more prejudiced people of all races in this world than one may think, and that it is really hard to change these opinions in others. I also learned a lot about the African American culture, which I feel is very important.

Now that I am in college in an entirely different city, it is a whole new experience. I think that in this smaller city the races are much more separated. I know that one may feel a smaller city would cause this to be the opposite, but through personal experiences and observations, I have noticed how things seem more segregated, but not on purpose. I feel many of the special clubs and organizations that are originally formed for the different ethnic groups to promote a positive association often produce separateness. I am not cutting these organizations down, because I feel that there are indeed many positive effects, but I think these groups should all be combined into one large group—a multicultural organization. I am aware that this exists on campus, but I feel that something needs to be worked on to collaborate all the individual groups. Multicultural awareness and sensitivity to other peoples' backgrounds are two very important issues to me.

I could go on and on about particular experiences I've had that were very important to my awareness of racism and prejudiced attitudes. I feel very fortunate to have the background that I have had and to be aware of this issue that is with us each day. I can only hope that multicultural education will be expanded in the future. I believe that this will be a key contributor to understanding and peace among the many different racial and ethnic groups on our planet.

SUMMARY

From these essays we see that the capacity for social distance or prejudice against other racial, ethnic, or religious groups develops in stages. Young children do not exhibit social distance against those who are different from them. The narrators tell us time and again how other-regarding they were to the children, whom their parents disdained. Children tend to react on a personal rather than on a group level. When aversions among children do arise, they usually stem from personality clashes between two individual children regardless of their differential background.

Later, during preadolescence and adolescence, the bulk of the prejudicial attitudes arise. During this time the child may hear his or her parents speak against certain groups. As he or she absorbs this home atmosphere, the child begins to make distinctions on a stereotypical, categorical basis rather than on the personal basis used previously. A number of essays, however, indicate that some children evaluate their judgment of others on a personal level, but this time they are also conscious of their parents' stereotypical judgment of others. This creates a psychological, and sometimes an interpersonal, conflict between children and parents on matters of race and ethnicity both at the ideological and the behavioral levels. Usually these distinctions do not come from the direct experience of the child with diverse individuals, but rather they come from generalizations formed by parents. The conflict experienced by the child is due to the fact that the parents practice verbal and actual xenophobia, while they preach ideal xenophilia. In many essays, the adolescents, under certain conditions, enlarge upon and express more strongly the value orientation learned from their parents. However, in other essays we see that the pressure of the child's peer group to see other groups in a manner different from that of the child's parents increases as the child interacts with more and more diverse peers.

Therefore, although the bulk of prejudicial attitudes are acquired at the preadolescent and adolescent periods, they continue into adulthood. Those children who are taught to judge others on a personal, rather than on a group level, will continue to do so into their adulthood. When they encounter any aversions, they regard them as personality clashes between themselves and that individual, regardless of the diversity of the individual's background. However, those children who have been given mixed messages in their lives will either conform to the power of their parents' equivocation and preach xenophilia while they practice xenophobia or they will snap out of their parents' hypocrisy and do what their conscience tells them, at the risk of exorcism or disownment.

4

In the Gym and Boardroom

In these essays people of different races and ethnic backgrounds encounter each other, sometimes for the first time, on the playground (gym) or at work (boardroom). In some essays different work ethics, due to cultural and socioeconomic differences, complement each other to accomplish a task. Also, we see the differential treatment of people based on skin color at workplaces such as shopping centers, banks, or big corporations. Access to housing, social services, and employment are also highlighted. Recreation as an American institution is not free from the issues of diversity and sociocultural conflict.

Greater interaction between Whites and minority groups at work and play highlights the prejudices that each group brings to the arena of interaction and separates the liberal idea from the conservative one about racial mixing. The narrators in these essays help us identify who the protagonists and antagonists are, thus proving to us that racial and ethnic conflict still plagues the American gym and boardroom. The narrators in these essays stand out in most cases not necessarily as "holier-than-thou" characters, but as participant players who have in one way or another had to face their own prejudices and those of others as they encounter persons who are different from them culturally, racially, and socioeconomically. Most of the narrators state the value of tolerance and bid to do something about making American society gentler and friendlier to diversity. Some suggest strategies for accomplishing this task, including rebellion against their past indoctrination regarding diversity, striking out, vouching support for diversity, and touching the "untouchables."

However, some of the narrators are overwhelmed by the prescriptions and proscriptions of society when it comes to stereotypes about other groups. These sometimes become self-fulfilling prophesies and by being realistic about the stigma or societal sanctions that might ensue from alternative behavior deviant from that of their value-groups, they would rather conform than conflict with their significant others—their parents or their in-group.

WE WORKED TO HELP THE POOR

The childhood impressions and attitudes toward those of different racial and religious groups that my family, my school, and other institutions instilled in me were very nonracial. I attended a small high school in an area where one Black family lived, whose child went to the same school as I. My family always taught me to treat everyone as I would want to be treated. My church also instilled the idea that everyone is equal no matter what the color of their skin. To my surprise, my community was very indifferent to what they believed in. They didn't like the idea of a Black family living in the neighborhood. The Black family who lived in the neighborhood was so poor that other members of the community felt that their residence was an eyesore that made the community look sloppy.

One experience I had with people of a different race and religious group was when I went on a church work camp to South Carolina. I remember that when we arrived at John's Island it was very run down. I remember the members of the community being very, very black. This was one of the first times I was away from my Door County residence, and I couldn't believe there was such poverty in the United States. We drove to the community center where we would be staying. Everyone in our group couldn't believe we were going to sleep there for seven days. The community center was a huge building with cement floors, and the only other room was the kitchen. The floors were filthy and the bathroom was outside. I remember feeling very uncomfortable with the surroundings in which I was forced to stay.

As soon as we had settled in the community center, there was a knock at the door. I think everyone's heart jumped. It was a local family who wanted to know what we White folk were doing there. When we explained that we were there to help rebuild and paint their homes and to start building a church, they couldn't understand why a bunch of White teenagers would want to spend a week of their summer helping people. The next couple of days were very different. I was uncomfortable working there. The members of the community just stared at us. At the time I wanted to say, "Hey, do you want to help us paint your house?" But I didn't. I just did what I was supposed to do. Then the third night we were there some of the neighborhood boys broke into the community center where we were staying and went through our suitcases. The funny thing was that they didn't steal anything. They just looked at what we brought along. The next day was the picnic where we and the members of the community all got together to play games and to talk. I'll never forget that day as long as I live. A little boy came up to me and grabbed my hand and said, "You know you're really lucky. You get to leave this damn place, but I'm stuck here forever. I'll be just like all of them with no place to work and no place to go to school. I'll just sit on the front porch all day." That was when I realized why they all just sat on the front porch and watched us work. They didn't know anything different. It's what they did every day of their lives. Later that day our group went into town and bought different supplies to help repair their homes. When we returned, we asked the owners of each home if they would help us. It was amazing. They said, "Yes!" We worked together and traded stories, and they asked us why we came to this place out of all the places we could have gone. We all answered that it was because we wanted to help people. It turned out to be a wonderful experience, and I learned about a different culture. I learned that just because someone may have a different skin color doesn't mean they are not just like me.

While attending college I have had many different opportunities to interact with persons of a different race. I lived in a residence hall for a year, and the girl next door to me was an African American. We spent a lot of time together sharing stories and talking about different things, about the society we live in. I have never personally been discriminated against. However, one Saturday afternoon my friend and I went shopping, and the sales clerk asked us if we would leave because my friend was disturbing the elderly couple in the store. I asked the sales clerk how my friend was disturbing the elderly couple, and she responded, "She's Black and they're White and they feel uncomfortable with a Black girl." I asked the store clerk if my friend were uncomfortable with the elderly couple would she ask them to leave? She was furious and so was I. I asked to speak with her supervisor and needless to say no one was asked to leave but the sales clerk. It was awful to experience this sort of treatment.

I believe everyone should be treated with dignity and respect. I may not wish to date or marry someone of a different race, but that doesn't mean I shouldn't respect someone who does. I am not a prejudiced person but I feel our society is, and that makes it very difficult for us to get along. Discrimination is still prevalent in the area of employment, education, and many other areas of our society. I believe it is really sad that in today's society we can fix things with lasers but we can't fix the relationships between racial groups. Our differences are the connection to the future, but if we don't maintain our relationships now, what will the future bring?

SLURS AT SOCCER AND WRESTLING

When I think back on my childhood, I remember very little about prejudice and racial slurs. My brother, sisters, and I were always told by our parents to treat people as we would like to be treated no matter what their race, color, or religion. I try to live my life by this credo.

I do not remember being told to treat people differently depending on their race, color, or religious preference in grade school (K–5). It was never talked about. Racial remarks were not used that much because there were not a lot of different people in my town. The only time I can remember any discussion about a person of a different race is when my travel soccer team was going to host another team from Virginia for the Memorial Day Weekend Tournament. It was the custom to billet visiting teams with local soccer players who were playing in the tournament. There was one Black boy on the Virginia team, and my family was the only White family that would agree to take him for the weekend. We had billeted before because my older brother and sisters also played in this tournament. Sometimes the players were really nice, sometimes they were not. My parents said that this was true with everybody and that race was not the reason. As it turned out, the Black boy that stayed with us was not nice. He was used to having his own way, his own room, and live-in help. When he wet the bed, he claimed it was because our roof leaked. We didn't enjoy having him stay with us, but we wouldn't have enjoyed him regardless of his color. He was a snob.

We moved to Illinois when I was in the sixth grade. It was at this time that I started to hear racial remarks. Once again, we did not live in a racially diverse community so racial remarks within my community were kept to a minimum. I had been wrestling since I was in second grade, and made the school wrestling team when I was in sixth grade. We traveled to other schools to compete. If we went to another school where there was a different ethnic or racial population, there were racial slurs and gestures. It made me feel uncomfortable to hear someone say things just to hurt someone else. Some of the comments made were stupid and unfeeling. For instance, if one of our wrestlers had to wrestle against a Black boy, often there would be a comment about his hair being greasy, his body being slippery, or his body having an odor. This continued from sixth through eighth grade.

When I went on to high school, I found it was not my high school friends who were making the racial comments, but rather their parents. During sporting events I heard remarks such as, "Look at the big nigger," or "You're going to wrestle the spic," or "Watch out, all Mexicans are tricky." My high school girlfriend's father always made remarks about the Jews and other groups of people. When she went to college, she began to sound like her father. I noticed that most of the children of these parents began to say the same things their parents said. Many of them continue to recite their parents' views to this day.

I went to Europe in my junior year to play soccer. The team was made up of soccer players from the Midwest, who had tried out and made the team. Most of us did not know anyone on the team prior to making the team. I do not know if it was because our team kept to itself, or if it was due to the fact that we were too busy trying to win our games to bother with unimportant prejudices, but I did not experience any prejudice there.

I have had several opportunities to know people of other races, religions, and nationalities. My sister went to college in North Carolina. One of her roommates was Black. My sister's friend came home with her for spring break one year. She was very nice and my whole family liked her. My sister met her husband while in college. He is a Muslim from Russia. He does things differently than we do, because of his religion and his nationality. For example, he neither celebrates Christmas nor eats pork. These things are not important. I enjoy talking with him and going to sporting events with him. We have a lot in common. My oldest brother is married to someone outside our religion. She is very nice and the different religion is not an issue. I do not know if I will date or marry someone of a different race or religion. It is not something I have given any thought to. I believe it would depend on the person and whether or not we are attracted to each other.

THE MAJORITY OF THE WORKFORCE WERE MINORITIES

The thing I remember most about my childhood socialization, concerning racial and ethnic stereotypes, is a general confusion as to what all the names, phrases, and stereotypes meant. The earliest recollection I have of the use of an ethnic slur is from my very early grade school years. Often when my family ordered out Chinese food, my parents would refer to it as "gook food." At first I thought "gook" was just a nonsense word. Then I thought it was just another word for Chinese food (like cantaloupe and muskmelon are the same thing). One day when I was about eight or nine, my sister yelled at my parents for calling it "gook food" and told them to just call it "Chinese food." I began wondering if "gook" was somehow a bad word. Then after hearing it in context on "M*A*S*H" a few times, I finally realized what it meant. I never thought of Chinese people as "gooks." I just wondered why my parents would want to use that word.

Another phrase my parents used a lot was "boogie bear country." My rough understanding of that phrase is a section of town where primarily Black people reside. I'm not sure if that is the right definition or if it only includes those areas of the city that are also fairly dangerous neighborhoods. I have never understood the illusion of "boogie bear country," but I can only assume it's derogatory.

My parents weren't the only source of my confusion though. I had a friend in high school who was prejudiced against Black people, but I think that her views came straight from her parents. Every time I asked her why she said or did something in reference to someone culturally different, she would always say something about the fact that that is what her parents always said. For example, we were walking home from the movies once, and a Black man was about a half block away and walking toward us on our side of the street. My friend suddenly wanted to cross the street and walk on the other side. Once again, I didn't understand why. I vaguely understood that she must have thought the Black man was dangerous for some reason, but I didn't know why she thought that. She crossed the street by herself, because I told her I wasn't going to walk on the other side of the street, unless she gave me a good reason why I should. I walked past the Black man—a little nervous, because I wondered if my friend knew something I didn't know, and more than that, I was a little ashamed of the childish way she was acting. When she crossed back to my side of the street after the man was gone, she told me that her mom always told her to stay away from Black people because you never know what they're going to do.

On another occasion, the same friend and I were in the locker room after gym class. There was a Black girl who had gym the same hour as we did but was in the special education class. A number of people made fun of her because she was quite retarded and "really weird" as far as most people were concerned. The retarded girl had done something to annoy my friend, and my friend came back to her locker ranting and raving about "that dumb little jig." "What are you talking about?" I asked her. "That weird jig girl." "Who?" "You know the weird Black girl?" "What on earth is a jig?" "A jig. A jigaboo." "I don't get it. What's a jig?" She replied, "I don't know. That's what my mom calls them."

It's probably fairly obvious that I never had much orientation with people of different cultures before I graduated from high school. I'm from a large middle-class suburb. It is apparently known for its lack of cultural diversity, a quality I had never noticed until it was pointed out to me. I was once told that I lived in a "good" neighborhood, because "there aren't any niggers living there," and on another occasion someone told me, "Oh yeah, I know where you live. They couldn't make room for none of the brothers there."

Before I went to high school, the only non-Whites I can remember knowing were the three Korean kids, who were adopted by the White family, who lived across the street from us. When I was a freshman in high school, we had two Black kids, who were bused from Milwaukee (the beginning of an effort to integrate the mostly White suburbs surrounding Milwaukee). Before the next school year, one was expelled because of disciplinary charges and the other, rumor has it, chose not to return. The latter was a con artist of the first degree, and he had apparently made a few, if not too many, enemies.

When I graduated, there were about six Black students, who attended our school. There was only one, who was in my grade, though. I didn't know her very well, but I remember always feeling sorry for her. She was in my cultural geography class, and by the misfortune of alphabetical seating, she ended up in the first row in the middle of the class, right in front of the professor. Being assigned a seat in that location was bad enough, but, in what I assume was his attempt to be nonracist, our professor constantly asked her questions about what it was like to be Black or always used her as an example, whenever we talked about cultural differences. If I were her, I would have hated that class and the professor as well.

To tell the truth, I don't know if we had any people of Hispanic background or any other non-European background who went to my school. For example, a girl I knew liked a guy in our grade named Joe. I remember someone saying something to the effect that he was cute even though he was a spic. My initial reaction was to cringe at the word "spic," but then I thought, "What does she mean a spic? Joe's not Hispanic. Well, wait a minute. His last name is Torres. His skin is a little dark. Maybe he is Hispanic. I never really thought about it." I never really paid attention to what ethnic background people belonged to. I noticed the Black students in our school, because I didn't know any of them. I knew the names of both of the students who left and the girl in my grade, but I didn't really talk to any of them very much. The more I knew someone culturally different, the less important it was that they were different. For example, the Black students I didn't know were "some Black kids." The Black girl in my grade was "Michelle, someone who is Black." The Korean girl, whom I've been friends with since she moved here in third grade, was just Sarah. When people referred to her as the "Oriental girl," it always took me a minute to figure out who they meant, because she was just Sarah to me.

I think it was Michelle, the girl in my grade, who first made me race conscious. She seemed nice, but I don't think she had many friends in our primarily White school. I always thought it would be neat to get to know her because I didn't know anyone Black, but I didn't know how to approach her. Then again, I was very shy in high school—I didn't know how to approach anyone. I wondered if she hated our cultural geography teacher, who always made an example out of her. I wondered what she thought of White people in general. I wondered if she thought I never talked to her because I was shy or because I was a White racist pig. I can't look at Black people and see what is wrong with them because they are Black, like some other White people might. I see them and wonder what they think is wrong with me because I'm White.

I think that if I had my choice of what race I'd like to be, I would still rather be White, but I'm not proud of being White. Most people who are ethnic or racial minorities are very conscious of their background and proud of that background. For example, I used to work with a young man who had a sweat shirt that read "The Blacker the college, the sweeter the knowledge." That statement would be considered to be something demonstrating racial pride. If it read "the Whiter the college, the sweeter the knowledge," though, it would be considered an example of racism and White supremacy. It's dangerous for the majority to be too proud of who they are. Or maybe we just have less to be proud of and more to be ashamed of.

According to some experts, anyone who is part of the majority and not actively working to change the status quo of society is actually being discriminatory. The impression I get is that by simply being part of the majority, I discriminate against minorities. If that is the case, I have no reason to be proud of being White. I know that some minorities look at me and only see the color of my skin. Some minorities see me as White and assume all of the things about me that I'm afraid they do—until they get to know me. I realize that unconscious racism is perhaps more prevalent than conscious racism; but with my White, middle-class values, I cannot understand how the problem is 100% the fault of the White majority nor how my being part of the White majority puts me at fault as well. I also think that this view of mine is probably the result of my ignorance and naivete and may change over time. There are a number of things I don't understand about minorities due to a sheer lack of experience with them.

Last summer I had an educational experience that made me understand a little more about what it is like to be a minority. When I go home during breaks, I usually end up doing temporary work in factories because those are the only places of business that will hire me for such a short period of time unless I want to flip burgers for a living. Last summer when I went home, I began working at a meat packing plant in a suburb on the north side of Milwaukee. The first time I walked into the break room, I never felt so uncomfortable about being White in all my life. Out of about sixty people who were sitting in there, I think I only saw about three White people—the majority of the workers at the plant were Black. Between the color of my skin and the Normal College sweatshirt I was wearing at the time, I stuck out like a sore thumb. Everyone stared at me when I walked in. I tried to act like none of what was happening had the slightest effect on me, but I admit I was nervous.

It didn't take me long to figure out that most of the people who worked there thought I was just a White college brat, who was completely spoiled, and who probably wouldn't make it through the first day. Most people were friendly to me, but by the things they said to me, I could tell they were laughing at me on the inside for thinking that I could possibly fit in there. Throughout the first week, most of the conversations I had with people consisted of them trying to feel out who I was and how I felt about Black people. For example, one man, who was working on my line, went outside during break and didn't hear our line called back to work. When he finally came back, he said to me, "You were outside, you knew I was out there, why didn't you come get me when they called us back?" I told him I wasn't paying attention to who was outside, and I didn't realize he was out there. He replied with a laugh, "Oh, I know all us Black guys look alike to you."

On another occasion, I was eating lunch with two young Black men, two constant sources of jabs about my being White. When John asked me what nationality I was, I started listing them off and got as far as German when he cut in with "Really, so am I. Oh, just kidding." After I finished my list of the six nationalities I am, he tried to start a discussion about how "White people, well some White people" always say that the White race is the pure race but there are all kinds of Whites so it's probably the least pure race. Before allowing me to answer he informed me that people have interracial relationships all the time and that there really is no way of knowing if each person is of one pure race just by looking at him or her. "So how can you all say that yours is the pure race when there aren't really any pure races?" he asked me. "Did I say that?" I asked him. "Well, no," he responded, "but White people say that all the time." "Listen, I said, I know there aren't any pure races. I never said there were. Ask somebody who thinks there are pure races." "Okay, okay," he said with a smile. Apparently he was satisfied for the moment, but it was a long time before he trusted me. The next Monday I was standing at my line working and John walked past and said, "You still here, I don't believe you came back. I never thought you'd last three days in this place."

John's friend Steve also said things to me when I first met him that would allow him to find out how I felt about different races—or more accurately, his statements made it sound as if he had already decided I was against Black people, and he was campaigning for his race. One day he was working with me and did something to help me out so I thanked him. "See, I'm not a jerk," he said. "A lot of Black guys are real jerks, but I'm not." "A lot of White guys are real jerks," I told him. "It doesn't really matter what color you are to be a jerk." "Yeah, I guess you're right," he said.

A couple of minutes later John came by, and they both started doing their White people impressions. They began talking in their California surfer accents and saying "dude" at least three times in every sentence. I started laughing hysterically. I'd never heard anyone do an impression of a White person before, and I thought it was one of the funniest things I'd ever heard. Steve and John both gave me strange and surprised looks. Then they started laughing too and asked me if anybody really talks like that. It suddenly dawned on me that they never expected me to laugh, and I wondered if all this time they were fooling around with me or really trying to insult me. I wondered if I had been Black and they had been White if I would have been really mad and have thought they were racist. I wondered if I blew off insults as jokes, because I really did think the White race is superior. Maybe I never thought twice about the jokes, because I'd never heard any White racist jokes and couldn't recognize one when I heard it. Or was it just my laissez-faire personality and pure naivete? I think blonde jokes are funny, too, because I don't really think that anyone could truly believe all those things are true about a person simply because she is blonde. From then on I never heard any more White jokes, but I was still bothered, wondering exactly why they said any of them in the first place.

The longer I worked there, the more comfortable I became working with a culturally different work force and the more comfortable the workers became with me. When I started working there, I learned what it was like for people to have misconceptions about me and not trust me because of the color of my skin. I also began understanding what it is like to be different from all of the other people around me. Except for the women in personnel and the security guard, who did not work in the plant itself, for most of the summer, I was the only White female that worked second shift. The people working with me also learned to like and trust me despite their previous convictions about White, middle-class, college students. Working there reinforced my beliefs that ignorance is the main cause of discrimination.

I don't want to be interracially ignorant. I want to learn how to live in a culturally diverse world and not have to feel uncomfortable about my background or anyone else's because they are ethnically, culturally, or racially different. For this reason, I am doing my intermediate field experience at the Normal College Black Center. It should be a valuable learning experience.

This paper by no means depicts all of my experiences and beliefs concerning race, ethnicity, and cultural differences. Race, ethnicity, and culture are all complicated issues that cannot be dissected and examined completely in such a short paper. I chose to talk about the things that stand out most in my mind. I think, though, that if I had to sum up my beliefs in one sentence, I would say that in order to curb prejudice and discrimination, people must learn how to look past what is different about other people's race, culture, and ethnicity and see those people as people and not as Black, Jewish, or Italian. As Michael Jackson said in his song, "Black or White, I don't want to spend my life being a color."

WE DON'T CASH WELFARE CHECKS HERE

Until the fourth grade, people of other ethnic groups and specifically Whites, only came to me through television. The medium with its channel trite depictions of the "All American" lifestyle left me with the feeling that the people of European descent dominate the TV waves and society in general. I've come to realize that

TV sitcoms have done White Americans just as much a disservice as they have African Americans. It promotes tolerance without understanding, without mutual dignity. It should promote so much more, especially when the number of worldwide viewers are taken into account.

Upon entering the fourth grade, I underwent desegregation or that state of anxious confusion a child undergoes when the state says, "Dammit, mingle and love each other!" My views were forever changed. On a daily basis, the issue of Black versus White was lived, rarely talked about, but always experienced. I've met some Whites who I will always love, others I will admire, others I am intrigued by, still others I despise. All of this is much the same way I both love and fear for my people. Love some, hate others.

When I entered college, I met people who were from far away—Africans, Middle Easterners, Asians, Laotians, and American Indians. Because these people are so underrepresented in American television, I had no real stereotypes of them. I just knew that they thought of us (Blacks) as dumb, undisciplined, promiscuous, vulgar, unruly, and dependent. This could be a stereotype on my part that they have stereotypes about Blacks.

I find myself wanting to talk to them, laugh with them, argue with them, let them hear Luther, Anita, and Public Enemy, share with them, be taught something significant by them as I teach them something significant. I want to go beyond Black versus White versus Asian versus African versus African American versus rich versus poor. Sometimes I cry when I think about the struggles I must face so that my children will not have to.

For example, one time I went to cash my payroll check at a store and was informed, "we don't cash welfare checks!" I work for the Federal Aviation Administration and there I overheard two men discussing the latest appointment to two Regional Administrator positions. One said to the other, "Did you hear they elected a 'Moulie' to Regional Administrator?"

When I was a child another child called me a nigger. The little boy's mother simply nodded nervously. Perhaps she didn't anticipate her son's repeating the word in public. The incidents stack up. I worked with a young Korean girl. I said she "talks White" because of her "valley girl" accent. When I finally got to know the young idealistic wanna-be-lawyer named Mary, I apologized. I knew it wasn't enough. She did not ask for my smart-assed comment just as I didn't ask to be called a nigger or mistaken for a welfare recipient, who should not be ashamed to be a welfare recipient. But the oppressed become the oppressor all too easily, and the ridiculed ridicule, because we know of no other way. But an oppressor is an oppressor, is an oppressor. When one of my favorite teachers looked at me one day and said, "Ms. G., I'll bet you're one of those people who don't know they're Black." I should have verbally put him in his place. I did not. He had the grade book. I only held my tongue and embarrassment. The teacher then proceeded to ask me why I "don't try and pass for White," but rested his case only after a "but your hair will never make it." An oppressor is an oppressor, is an oppressor.

REVERSE DISCRIMINATION

During my early childhood, I was raised to believe everyone was equal. My mother taught me that a human being is important no matter what color he is. People are people, we all have the same thoughts and feelings.

I don't remember hearing about or seeing any Black people until I was twelve years old. I remember being a little afraid of "those Black kids." It wasn't anything my parents told me. Actually, the only thing my parents said was that Blacks are okay people in their place. By this they meant that they were okay as long as there was no dating between Blacks and Whites. It was fine otherwise to socialize. I picked up my fears from school and the things kids said about Blacks. They would say things like: "Blacks fight in groups," "If you get the Blacks mad at you, the whole group is after you," "Blacks are really tough," "The Black boys really like the White girls and this leads the Black girls to hate you," "Blacks are troublemakers," "Don't look at the Blacks because they will just use that as an excuse to beat you up," "Blacks fight dirty—with knives." These are just a few of the things I can remember.

Now I realize those kids were just repeating the prejudices they learned from their parents and possibly their friends, and not actually from experience. At that time a lot of school kids came to our house. All the kids liked my parents and of course us children too. So the Black kids came to our home. They ate supper with us in the same manner as the White children did. They had good manners and said "please" and "thank you" like anyone else. So I decided they were just people.

When I was sixteen, I worked at Kentucky Fried Chicken. My boss was a Black man. He had a White girlfriend. At that time, I felt real strange about that situation, because of my parents' ideas that the two don't go together. I got used to it and I thought, "Well, to each his own." I saw nothing wrong with Blacks dating Whites. I think a person's heart, not the color of his skin is important. But because of the way I was raised or maybe it's just personal preference, I would not date a Black man. Maybe it is a type of prejudice but I don't think so. I'm not attracted to dark skin. That includes Indians, Mexicans, and Italians. So I think it's more a personal preference. It's like how some people wouldn't go out with someone who is too skinny, too fat, or someone who smokes.

I haven't had any negative experiences with Blacks. My experiences with Blacks have all been positive. Blacks have suffered from discrimination and economic deprivation far longer than any other American ethnic group. Sometimes I think we wouldn't realize Blacks were Blacks and Whites were Whites if society wasn't there to remind us or tell us in the first place. I have a Black friend who told me that when she was in third grade she had a boyfriend. They played together all the time. Their families associated together. They were holding hands at school one day, when the teacher took them in the hallway, and told them they couldn't hold hands anymore. She told my friend that she was Black and the little boy was White and Blacks and Whites don't touch each other. My friend said she was devastated. She cried and cried. She said she didn't know Black from White. She didn't realize they were different from one another because her society didn't recognize those differences. But leave it to one prejudiced school teacher to ruin everything—to point out differences that were seen by her, not by the kids or their families. Society has a huge impact on the things we do or don't do.

As an adult now, I work with Blacks and I've gone to school with them. I feel there are no differences. Oh sure, they talk differently and some things vary but as people we are alike. We have the same wishes, hopes, dreams, and we have the same feelings. Yes, you have lower-class, undereducated Blacks. But there are Whites in the same boat. These days I can't help but think there are as many underprivileged Whites as there are Blacks.

There are large numbers of White people who are on welfare, homeless, and jobless. It seems that for years Blacks have been prejudiced against. There has been program after program to help Blacks. What about Whites? It's almost like reverse prejudice to some degree. Who helps the Whites get the jobs, the education? If you're White and rich, you get it all. If you're White and poor, it's too bad. If you're Black and poor, you're a minority and you qualify for more than those in the "White and poor" category. The Blacks qualify for the same student loans that Whites do. There are also funds for Blacks at certain colleges. There are also colleges for Black people—these schools make it nearly impossible for Whites to get in.

As an adult I've seen Black people use "prejudice" as a crutch—an excuse. If a Black person doesn't get the job they want, they cry prejudice. If the boss reprimands them on the job—it's prejudice. If they don't get the grades they want or the evaluation they want—it's prejudice. I know Whites have excuses too. I'm personally tired of the word "prejudice" in relation to Black people. The slave days are over, no one alive today was a slave. Why carry the torch? Maybe when I do my next research paper, I'll do it on Black prejudice.

A MULTICULTURAL WORKPLACE

I grew up in a rural community and don't remember thinking a whole lot about people being different. I grew up during the civil rights movement. As a small child I don't remember much about that besides what I learned in later years in history class. I don't remember my parents talking about racial differences or having curiosities. The only thing I do remember is that the Negroes had their own part of town on North Main Street. I do remember these people were referred to as "niggers." My dad had some friends in this part of town whom he used to hunt with or take me to visit. He always said of them: "They like that kind of stuff—beef hearts, tongue, sweet breads, greens, etc." I never realized any difference though. I went to a country school one year, then to a private Catholic school for four years. I was always pretty much segregated from anyone that was different from me.

I remember growing up hearing my aunt, a Protestant, talking about those Catholic kids always being in trouble. Her kids went to public school and were by no means angels either.

I remember my father, after he started working in the city (instead of farming), talking on occasion about how lazy the Black man at work was. My mom would respond that "there are lazy White men too." I believe all people should be treated equally, given a fair chance at whatever they want to do, and not be denied a job because of race, religion, or other discriminatory grounds if they are qualified for the job. But sometimes a Black woman will be hired in a spot as a "token" to fulfill needs of both race and sex discrimination.

Since coming to college, I have been exposed to more differences outside of my community. It seems that PAYE has a variety of races on campus. I find it interesting where these different people, who speak differently from me, come from. I am quite fascinated at how they ended up in Little Dixie. The group who was in my English class last semester (my culture was in the minority) consisted of a mixture of other cultures—one-third of the students were from Micronesia, off the Hawaiian Islands. The others were from Nigeria. I think the instructor was a little hard on some of the students from Micronesia. She seemed to ask them a lot of questions. They did not seem to understand what she was talking about. She became quite angry one day when a student did not respond to her question and lashed out at the student. I don't know how the student felt. She just sat there, kind of stunned.

I have worked with a variety of people. I give them a fair chance on occasion. I work with a registered nurse and pharmacist (husband and wife) who are of some Oriental nationality, I'm not sure which one. The only problem I have working with them is a communication variance. I don't understand them, and they don't always understand me. It seems like other employees are kind of hard on them. Because they speak differently, they always look for things to go wrong.

Whenever I am around someone of a different race, I think as if I were blind and ask myself if I would react differently if I could not see him. Usually my answer is that I would not know the difference. I have a good friend who is Black whom I really enjoy working with. There are some WASP people whom I work with that I don't consider friends but I tolerate having to work with them.

There are still some ideas that stem from the era I was brought up in. Some of these are my parents' ideas that cause some unintentional discrimination on my part—the main one being interracial marriage. I would never do that. Otherwise I don't feel I have a problem with prejudice.

BASKETBALL PLAYERS ON A PEDESTAL

When I think back to my conservative childhood, I remember the first time I saw someone who had a different skin color. I was curious but I did not obsess about the color difference. Even though there were no people of color in my schools or town, my parents brought me up not to discriminate against any person who is any different from me.

The issue of racism and discrimination did not become an issue in my life until I started high school. I am not sure if I was exposed to people who came from different family backgrounds or if other students were trying to prove that they were ignorant of any person different from them. Some students, not many, used derogatory terms against the African American and Hmong populations in our area. At the time, I did not have the courage to speak up against such comments which included the use of the "n" word. We had one African American person in our school, and a large population of Hmong students, who other students criticized for being American citizens. Students believed Hmong families should not get welfare assistance or drive better cars than the students themselves were driving. Like I said, I did not know how to defend myself, much less a population of people I knew nothing about.

Somewhere along the way during my high school years, I became friends with many Hmong students. I helped them with the English language, ate lunch with them, and talked with them on a daily basis. At first I may have done this because I felt bad for them. But once I became friends with them, I did it because they were nice to be friends with. One incident I remember very clearly was at my hotel job. An angry person came to the front desk and wanted to complain to a manager. I observed with disbelief as the furious customer said, "There is no way that my family or I are going to swim in your pool. There is a n——r in there. They should not be able to swim in the same pool that my family is paying to swim in!" I could not believe my ears. My manager was quick to reply to the man that everyone was welcome in the same pool and then he asked the man to leave the hotel. I was amazed that there are still people who discriminate as if the days of slavery still existed. This man's view was extremely ethnocentric. At the time I did not know the meaning of the word, but now I know he fits the description of people who believe that their own culture is superior. This view has led to many of the worst atrocities in history.

Another group I remember hearing derogatory comments about are Native Americans. I remember the major fishing controversy in my state a few years ago. People became violent because Native Americans followed different fishing and hunting regulations.

When I moved to California it became much easier to be around people of different ethnic backgrounds. In Southern California there are so many different groups of people that I was in the minority. I became friends with many people whom I worked with, and their company helped me deal with the conservative lifestyle that I grew up with in my home state. Although it seemed discrimination was less of a problem in California, I still heard comments from angry people about the Mexican population moving over the Mexico-California border and "stealing American jobs."

When I started my college career, it helped me to understand people who came from different cultures, families, and belief systems. It was always so wonderful to hear everyone's story of where they came from and how they got to where they are today. It opened a window to my world that was never opened before. The world was so much larger and exciting than I ever imagined. My classmates who shared stories with me were also amazed at where I came from because I started college in California and when I told them that I was from Wisconsin, they thought *everyone* was a farmer. Hopefully I opened a new window to the world for them also.

There is a not so overt way Americans treat African Americans differently. For example, we tend to place African American basketball players on a hero pedestal. While this may sound complimentary, there is a danger that people will start to believe that capacities such as intelligence, morals, and work productivity are also determined by a person's race. This feeds into a negative view of African Americans.

I have never been a prejudiced person but I have to be honest and say I would have doubts about marrying a person from a country such as Iraq, Iran, or Russia. The fears I have about these countries were learned from the media. I have heard how men treat their wives in these countries with disrespect and violence. My goal now is to learn more about these countries since I have only been exposed to the negative views. Hopefully this will eliminate my negative thoughts of the men in these countries. Of course for the past five years, since I started college, I no longer stand by and just listen to discriminatory remarks. I react instantly.

A LASTING IMPACT FROM HABITAT FOR HUMANITY

I grew up in a small village in Wisconsin, populated entirely by Whites, where everyone knows everyone else. Throughout my childhood years, I was rarely exposed to people of another race or nationality. The only time I really was exposed to other races or nationalities was when my mom and I traveled to Milwaukee on a shopping trip. Because of this, when I was a child I associated Milwaukee with Blacks and other minorities. This is an example of a childhood socialization that led me to associate Blacks with Milwaukee along with the bad crime that plagues Milwaukee. I feel that my childhood associations have led me to hold certain prejudices of Blacks and other minorities to this day. Although, as I have grown, I have learned to overlook some of these prejudices and realize that they are people just like myself.

There was one particular event that sticks in my mind. I was a junior in high school. There was a group of about fifteen of us from my hometown church who went to Milwaukee to take part in Habitat for Humanity. For this project we traveled to 35th and Center streets in Milwaukee to build and remodel houses for less fortunate families. This area of the city, populated primarily by Blacks, was high in crime.

I can remember traveling down there with a feeling of great fear that I or one of my group members could be shot, mugged, or kidnapped. As we drove down to Milwaukee I experienced conversations that included various racial comments—for example, joking statements such as "What are we gonna eat for lunch, chicken and ribs?" Throughout the day, various other jokes and comments were made. This project was quite an experience for me because I had never really been exposed to this type of neighborhood before. There was a constant sound of emergency sirens, poorly clothed and unsupervised children running about, streets filled with trash, and houses that were in terrible condition. This being the first time I was exposed to living conditions such as these made me very thankful for my family and home life. This experience left a very lasting impression on me, not to the extent of causing me to possess a racial outlook, but just to realize how some people have to live unfortunate lives.

My opportunities in college to meet and get to know people different from myself in race and nationality have been rather limited. This has to do with attending a primarily White college. I would like to broaden my horizons and get to know people of other races and ethnic groups. Some sort of fear within me makes me feel intimidated by people different than myself, but I feel in order to overcome my fear I must begin to get to know them. I feel that this fear was instilled in me because of growing up in a predominantly White village.

About the dating issue?! I, myself, would and have considered dating someone of another race or ethnic group. My philosophy is as long as you are happy with this person and they make you happy it should be no one else's concern. As far as my parents are concerned, my mom wouldn't mind the dating part at all, but she may show a little more negative concern for marriage. As far as my dad, I think he would be disturbed by the whole thing regardless of whether I was dating or marrying someone of a different race. I think he would be embarrassed. My brother, on the other hand, hasn't approved of anyone I have ever dated so it really wouldn't matter. These feelings that my family possesses, I feel, have a lot to do with the village and family backgrounds we have. Neither one of my parents is the type to lash out at people of other races or ethnic groups. My family has its own opinions on this particular issue, like others do too.

On the other hand if I were to go out and continue what I wanted to do regardless of what my family thought, I know that they would not alienate me because of my decision. I think that is a very important aspect.

In conclusion, I feel that we need to begin to handle racism like adults. It has been going on for far too long, and I feel that we need to come to our senses in certain aspects. A lot of the racial tension, I feel, is rather immature. We need to somehow overcome the fears that we may have toward other races and ethnic groups, that may be the causes of these tensions, so we can all begin to live a peaceful life.

WORK TO HELP THE DISADVANTAGED GROUPS

When reflecting upon my experiences with people of other racial groups, I see myself making more contact the older I get. I have been born and raised in Lacustrine City, which a predominantly White, middle-class city. My family and I do not stray from this norm at all, so making contacts with people of other racial backgrounds has not been easy for me. It was not until I enrolled in college that I had such an opportunity. Let me take you on a short, chronological tour of my life and the influence people of other races have had on me and the effect I have had on them.

Let's begin by looking at my childhood, and the ways that my family and schools influenced my opinions about people who did not look like me. As I have said before, growing up in Lacustrine City gave me very few opportunities to meet others of different races. In fact, I do not remember anyone who was not White in my elementary school. The only time I can recall seeing non-Whites was when my family traveled to another city or went on vacation. Despite my lack of exposure to people from other races, I was not taught any forms of racism. In all actuality, I was taught to be extremely accepting of others, no matter what our differences. I was also taught to learn from these differences, and that they could enhance my life. These values were consistently instilled in me by my school and my family.

The first opportunity I had to interact with other races was after elementary school. This was the time I spent in middle school and high school. The predominant racial group who I was able to be involved with was Asian, specifically Hmong students. To me this was not a difficult transition because of the things I had been taught earlier. To enhance what I had previously learned, I do not recall ever seeing any negative qualities displayed by the Hmongs whom I had contact with. All were good students and contributed to the quality of our school in extracurriculars. Beyond the personal achievements of the Hmong students, they contributed to broadening my perspectives on world events. The tragedies and injustices that they had suffered made me see that I was not living in a perfect world. I am grateful for my first experiences with people of another race. They were positive and helped me gain knowledge I may not have otherwise known.

The other racial group that I had contact with at this time were the Mulattoes. This was definitely an easy group for me to associate with, because in every way, except that half their heritage was Black, they were exactly like me. We had all grown up in the same area and because of this we all had the same cultural values. Maybe our skin was a slightly different shade, but besides that, we did not have any differences.

The years I have spent in college have been the greatest chance for me to interact with people of other races. The people I have encountered with different racial backgrounds have been professors, students, and clients I have had. It is quite ironic that I am still living in the same city that I grew up in, but I have much more exposure to a racial mix.

My first interactions with other races at Normal College were with professors. I have had Hispanic, Asian, and Black professors. While in the classes they teach, I have heard negative comments about some of these professors. Many times it was not the style of teaching that the professor possessed that students criticized, but rather they criticized how different the professor was. They did so without understanding cultural and racial differences. It would be wonderful to say that we are in a university community that is free of racial tensions, but just from sitting in on a class taught by a non-White professor, it is clear that this is not true. I have studied in the departments of Spanish, International Studies, and Latin American Studies. These are all areas that are truly enhanced by professors from other parts of the world. Our university would not have a perspective on world events if these professors did not bring it to us.

When it comes to my interaction with non-White students on campus, I find the situation a bit confusing. I personally do not see much discrimination among students, but I also do not find much mixing of racial groups. I have many acquaintances who are Black, Hispanic, Asian, or Middle Eastern, but I do not have any close friends from these groups. What I have seen on this campus is each group "sticking to their own." I find people of different races communicating in classes and during school activities, but outside of that, I do not see much companionship. I can see why people are comfortable with other people of the same racial and cultural background, but why have we not taken it any further than that?

Everything that I have learned and experienced involving other races has helped me to choose my areas of study here at Normal College. I am a Spanish and Human Services major. These areas of study give me the opportunity to work with disadvantaged Hispanics. This brought me to work for United Migrant Opportunity Services this summer. This was the most involvement I have ever had with someone from a different racial background. All of my clients were Mexican or Mexican American. I worked in an office where I was the minority as a White person. I knew the language and culture of my clients and co-workers, but obviously not as well as they did. This put me in a couple of awkward situations. For the first time, I knew what it felt like to be the minority. I also experienced, for the first time, how much discrimination there is in our community. Being the minority was not extremely difficult for me. The people I worked with were more than patient with me, and were extremely grateful for anything I could do for them. They have been a minority the entire time they've been in this country, and did not want me to feel out of place when I was in that position.

Realizing how much discrimination there is in this community was the other awkward situation I was put in. I dealt with employers, landlords, shelters, and social service agencies. All areas showed me and my clients one form of discrimination or another. Of course, it was never blatant or easy to prove, but we knew it was there. Many times I was given the sentiment that my clients should just go back to Mexico. Did these people truly comprehend how much food was being put on their tables by my clients' work? Did they understand the price increases or shortages of food they would face if my clients went "back to Mexico"? Many times I found it advantageous to be White when I had to face these discriminatory people. As much as I did not like what was occurring, I believed I could get more for my clients from the community, simply because I was White. Many times it took some educating about migratory families and the lives they were forced to live. Many days I was relieved to go home where everyone spoke English and had the same cultural values as I did. I am not saying that I did not appreciate the people I was working with and their culture, but it was different to be surrounded by unfamiliar things. Now I know exactly what my clients and many other minorities face everyday in this country.

I am very grateful for everything I have been taught by my family, my schools, and people of other races about the world we live in. My life has definitely been enriched by these people and the situations I have encountered. My next step is to spend six weeks in Mexico over interim. There I will be attending school, living with a Mexican family, and teaching Mexican children English. Further into the future, I plan to continue to help disadvantaged Hispanics by attending law school and then practicing public-interest law. I believe my past has prepared me well for what I face in the future, but I cannot wait to experience even more with people of other racial groups.

PLAYING TAG AND BASEBALL

I grew up in a small town in northwestern Wisconsin and lived there for my entire life prior to coming to Lacustrine City for college. If you've ever been to northwestern Wisconsin you'd know that it is a predominantly White area. Living there throughout my life, I didn't have much contact with other racial groups.

I remember first learning of other racial groups through television. I grew up watching a lot of sporting events on TV. My memory of how I first learned of this is not very clear, partially because I don't believe it was ever a very important issue in my life. The same is true with religious groups. I am Catholic, some of my friends are Lutheran or Methodist, but these are all similar. There was not a lot of diversity in the small town that I grew up in. Growing up I did hear a lot of derogatory phrases, mostly about African Americans, but at that point in my life—at the age of about ten—I didn't think anything of it. One example is when the neighborhood kids would play a game of tag or something like that to see who would be "it" first. We had a rhyme that went like this, "eeny meeny miney moe, catch a 'nigger' by the toe." The "n" word somehow was put into this phrase and that's how everyone said it. A good thing did come of this though. I was recently home visiting my family and my six-year-old nephew started saying a similar rythme, but instead of using the "n" word, he used "tiger" instead.

Another thing I remember as a child was visiting my aunt and uncle in Milwaukee. My uncle is a dentist, and they live quite well. He took my brothers and me to some Brewer baseball games as kids, and I remember leaving a game once and traveling through the inner city of Milwaukee. My uncle said, "Look you guys, this is where the 'brothers' live," referring to the African Americans. These are a few of the derogatory phrases that I've heard growing up. I do have some friends who still live in my hometown who haven't been anywhere else. When I go back, they do talk negatively about African Americans, but I feel that this is the way they were raised, and not getting out of the town doesn't help. This is the only way they know how to act, in which case they should probably stay there. I'm not saying that it's right that they say this, but I feel it's better that they just say it to themselves than to someone it would hurt.

Since starting college four years ago, I have had the opportunity to have some relationships with people of other races, but not of other religions. While playing baseball, I met and talked occasionally to an African American. He was the only non-White player on the team, and was probably one of the nicer players on the team. My sophomore year I became good friends with two African Americans who lived on my floor in the dorm. We did quite a lot of things together that year, and I still go out with, and talk to, both of them occasionally. An example of taking a person of a different race to my home hasn't happened yet. However, my friends in the dorms invited me to a cabin in northeastern Wisconsin for the weekend. They also asked Red, our African American friend on the floor, to go. His roommate and best friend, who is White and a high school friend of his, was already going. Red's first reaction was, "No way, I know what will happen to me up there." He was half joking and half serious, as he did expect to be looked at and talked about there, but on the other hand he was going with about fifteen friends from school (all of whom were White) who wouldn't stand for anything to be said about it or to him that weekend. During the trip there was only one small confrontation with a drunk man in one of the taverns. He said something that I didn't hear and one of my friends did. My friend went up to the man and asked him if he had a problem with Red, and if he did, then he had a problem with all of us. He didn't say another word.

If I fell in love with a woman, it wouldn't matter what race or religion she was. I have dated an African American girl while in school, but it never got very serious, mostly due to the pressure she got from her Black male friends. I think there are definitely some people out there who are against this, but if you're in love, color or religion shouldn't matter.

I don't think I've ever really been around other races long enough to understand all the differences that keep them separated. I've been sheltered in the small town that I grew up in.

SUMMARY

These essays show that the stereotype of minorities and the definitions of "proper" behavior toward them is depicted both in work and play situations. More and more Americans are working in multicultural environments. These environments are not only made up of the traditional American minority groups such as African Americans and Native Americans but also recent immigrants of non-European origins. In a way, these multicultural environments have fostered a better understanding of other cultures and ways of life. At the same time, the workplace is also breeding intercultural conflict. This stems from perceptions of fairness and access to jobs. Many Whites are becoming resentful of the opportunities that are created to attract minority groups in the workplace. There is also some disenchantment on the part of racial minorities. Those who work are accused of taking away jobs from Whites. Those who do not work are accused of being lazy.

Some of the essayists in this chapter also grapple with the pervasiveness of prejudice, especially toward minority individuals, whom they personally reach out for, regardless of the norms on which they were raised. These essayists have taken on an enormous crusade to change the behavior, if not of their parents, at least of themselves.

5

Higher Learning

In these essays the narrators give both sides of the role school plays in racial and ethnic relations. On the one side school, just like the family, the workplace, and the gym, helps dramatize and transmit the stereotypes and prejudices of society through generations. In this regard, narrators give us episodes of differential treatments that some students receive because of their master and ascriptive statuses. In most cases the school is the place where students and their teachers play out the prejudices that they bring with them from their families.

On the other hand, the narrators describe the progression of their education as a dialectical transfiguration of their values from the prejudices of home to a more enlightened and rationalistic appreciation of diversity. To many, the experiences at school and college expose them to the reality of diversity for the first time, dramatize it, and work as a laboratory where they are immersed in the experience of diversity, so that they gather enough data to base their new conclusions about diversity on new premises. Some clench their fears and the stereotypes they had before, but many cleanse their views and find diversity rich and reassuring. Basically, education is a liberating process because at school and college students of diverse groups are brought into close first-hand interaction.

These essays prove that casual contact with an ethnic minority will not necessarily lessen prejudice to the extent that intimate, equal-to-equal relationships with members of an ethnic group will. In order to counteract the ethnic stereotypes, the close, firsthand interactions that college offers are required. This type of relationship will lead to distinctions on the individual difference level rather than on the group stereotype level. Even where there is repeated contact, the modification of ethnic stereotypes is not likely to occur unless there is a reduction of social distance. The parents who have less contact with diverse groups than their children, who experience diversity in higher learning will retain prejudices, while their children will change perceptions for the better. This is because every contact with someone different from oneself affects prejudice positively or negatively. A person having no contact would gain no new information other than secondhand reports, which usually uphold tenacious stereotypes.

METAPHOR OF LIFE

Reflecting upon my cultural journey, three experiences come to the forefront. The first trail was short and extremely rocky. It happened while I was a child in elementary school. The second was a slow and gradual path that lead to enlightenment. I was a young adult whose house was shared with exchange students. The third was an overgrown section that needed work and maintenance. It took my adult life and a trip to a summer camp to do this. Each part of the journey has given me an insight into a better understanding of cultural diversity.

My first experience with racial diversity was while I was in fourth grade at the age of ten. My class was blessed with a wonderful young student-teacher. He introduced us to racism through "The Great Nerd Experiment." After reading and studying differences among cultures, our teacher chose several people to be the "nerds." I was one. My best friends were not. A large black "N" was drawn on the tops of my hands. I thought I was special.

Then it started. With little explanation, the experiment took off like a rocket. Suddenly, I was prohibited from sitting at my desk. I had to stand, in the back of the room. My books and other items were placed on the floor by my feet. The other nerds stood next to me. When the bell rang for recess, the rest of the class was instructed not to have any contact with the nerds. We were told to go outside and stay against the back fence until recess was over. During recess, the news spread quickly about The Great Nerd Experiment. My younger sister, who was in the first grade, came near the back fence, where I was standing. "Why are you standing here?" she asked. "I am a nerd," I replied. "What's that?" she questioned. Just then, the recess supervisor yelled at her to move away from the nerds. My closest friends started chanting and taunting us. The supervisor did nothing. The bell rang. All the children ran to get into line. The nerds also ran. I was hoping the experiment would be over when we got inside. As I approached the door, I noticed the recess supervisor was checking hands. Any student with an "N" had to return to the end of the line. Once inside, I headed to the restroom to wash the "N" off my hands. When I reached the door, a huge sign was posted on the outside that read "No Nerds Allowed." Our teacher made no remarks about what took place during recess. He was also oblivious to the names the nerds were being called. I also noticed a change in his vocal tonation when he spoke to us. I did not like it. At lunch, the nerds were the last students in the entire school to be served. Once served, we had to eat standing up because it was time for the custodians to prepare for the next gym class.

Frustrated and ready to burst into tears, I could not finish my lunch. Our teacher approached the far corner of the gymnasium. "It's over!" he said. We all went back to class. Little did I realize that those events would replay in my mind throughout life.

Through this experiment, the entire class learned what racism is and the effects it has on people. I learned a great deal more. Having been treated very poorly by people who were kind to me hours before taught me to question true friendship. I also learned that peer pressure is incredibly powerful. It is easy for the majority to gang up on the minority. I also learned that people tend to join in because they want to "be part of the action." In the case of The Great Nerd Experiment, it seemed that regardless of a person's age or position, the majority enjoyed having power over the minority. The nerds became my support system. The other "chosen" students were kids I would not have normally hung around with. We needed each other.

People are people and must stick together. We need to see the big picture. We are all in this together. I have become very cognizant of racism. It often fascinates me how my mind remembers, and takes me back to the old schoolyard.

Seven years later, when I was in high school, I ran across my grade school teacher. We chatted about The Great Nerd Experiment. He never did it again. I asked him why he stopped the experiment after lunch that day. He explained that a tiny little first grader, with tears streaming down her face, came up to him, tugged on his pant leg and said, "I used to like you, but now I hate you because you made my sister a nerd."

Unfortunately, there are not enough first graders to run and tug on each pant leg that needs tugging. Maybe some could yell, "It's over!"

When my sisters and I moved out of my mother's house, she started taking in foreign exchange students who attended the community college in our hometown. Each student stayed in our community for two years to complete an associate degree before returning to their home country. These students came from Haiti, Guatemala, El Salvador, and the Dominican Republic. All the exchange students spoke little, if any, English when they arrived, and we spoke virtually none of their language. Communication was definitely a hurdle. Together we became educated on the differences between our cultures.

I learned a great deal from each of our visitors. My observations are what taught me the most. None of the people had seen many of the "modern technologies" that we take for granted. For example, the students needed to be taught how to use a vacuum cleaner, a microwave oven, and a stove; one was amazed by the refrigerator. She never ate leftovers because in her country food did not keep overnight. When the refrigerator was explained, she was still very skeptical. The television set became a focal point to many of the students. They watched programs and rented movies to assist in learning English and the American culture. It was clear that many of our stereotypes from Hollywood were misunderstood by the guests.

The male versus female roles were interesting. Since my mother lived alone, she did all the maintenance and yardwork around the house. She strongly believed that to be part of a family everyone must chip in to do their part. Problems arose when my mother would ask the male students to clean, vacuum, cook, or do their laundry. The students' attitudes were obvious while doing such tasks. To them it must have seemed like "women's work." It was not clear to me at the time, but maybe it is possible that taking "orders" from a female was not their normal practice. The female students, on the other hand, were more willing to help in any capacity. They would help stack wood, rake the yard, cook their meals, and anything else to assist my mother. When my sisters and I came home, the students thought it strange that we all had cars, lived far away, and were not married. Their perceptions were that our family was wealthy and they were servants rather than part of the family.

Since my mother lived in a large, old, Victorian home, in an older section of town, the students thought she had a lot of money. They noticed she worked daily at the hospital, often double shifts. They also understood she was a health care nurse and cooked meals for an elderly gentleman. In her spare time, she worked in a neighboring emergency room. I believe that seeing the female work long hours was natural for these students. I think that cultural differences at times drove each person into real frustration. It was only after each started taking notice of the other's culture that the frustrations calmed.

Camp Tapawingo has been my summer home for the past twelve seasons. It is a residential, eight-week summer camp for girls age seven to fifteen. The ethnic background of these young ladies is predominantly Jewish. They reside in New York, Boston, Miami, Philadelphia, and Chicago. The counselors, on the other hand, are of the various Christian faiths and reside in many smaller communities across the country. One summer, there were two counselors of the Mormon faith.

These fellows talked openly about their beliefs and discussed with others the differences between the Jews, Christians, and Mormons. The older campers explained the Jewish traditions and history. The Christian and Mormon counselors contributed their understandings and beliefs. It was during this summer that I was educated as to why people believed so strongly in their religion, with little room for any other.

I was told about the various holidays, foods, prayers, and important people in each religion. Stories and information were shared with a sense of pride and strong feeling toward religious beliefs. Each person thought their religion was the "right" one. As I watched and thought about the discussions, I learned that people mainly believe what they believe through many years of dictated information. Since many of the participants in the discussion had never heard the foundations of other religions, they were very closed minded.

I found that each religion was soundly grounded. It was a sight to see people of different religions working together during the day and trying to understand others' points of view during the night. They all held their faith strong and truly believed in their teachings. Unfortunately, only a few felt the beauty of the moment that allowed minds to open.

In conclusion, although my cultural journey is a continuous process, I am grateful for the three paths that set a foundation for my future travels. My experiences have at times been negative, but the understandings gained have been positive.

Our country should be recognized as a vegetable soup where each vegetable adds its flavor to the whole. The soup would not be palatable if it was all one ingredient. The "melting pot" idea will never work. That would be like taking our vegetables and turning them into a puree. That would be a waste of wonderful produce.

SHE NEVER SPOKE ABOUT IT AGAIN

In reflecting on my childhood socialization, the impression, attitudes, and experiences I have had with members of other races and ethnic groups, I must come to the conclusion that I have had conflicting experiences concerning values that my family and certain social institutions have tried to instill in me. I have had few experiences with other cultures and races, but those experiences have made a substantial impact on my life and my attitudes concerning others and their differences.

As a native of Marshfield, Wisconsin, I moved at the end of the second grade to remote Pittsville, Wisconsin. The majority of the population I came into contact with were Caucasian Americans. Because of this, I think, as a child I failed to notice racial and ethnic differences in my peers.

In high school there was very little diversity. With a population of 300 to 400 students, I can recall one African American student (who was adopted) and five Native Americans who, at one time or another, attended our high school when I did. I also remember two foreign exchange students who I came to be close friends with. Lydia was from Mexico, and Hiroko was from Japan. Though they were few, my experiences and the relationships I had with several of these peers of various cultures and races, I think, played a strong role in forming the attitudes I have today concerning peoples from various racial and ethnic groups.

Even though I learned much from these individuals about accepting others and their differences, unfortunately, I had also been exposed to the prejudices of peers, family members, and others. I can distinctly remember my father stating (in regard to homosexuals, African Americans and Hmongs) that "we should just ship them all off to an island." He insisted that these people did not deserve the benefits America had to offer and that they would ruin society with their improper ways. I also recall him attending a meeting to protest Indian spear fishing. He proudly showed the newspaper article that contained the picture of him and my younger sister listening to the speakers at the protest while he tried to explain the issues to my sister, who was perched atop his shoulders. Being the avid fisherman he is, I truly believe he thought the treaties and spear fishing were unfair to the other outdoorsmen.

I also remember my stepfather spouting stereotypes about African Americans. He would always refuse to watch television shows with African Americans in them. On the other hand, my mother seemed to think his prejudice invalid, which made me think so as well.

In addition, I believe that the schools and churches had conflicting values they were attempting to instill. For example, the ideas that everyone is equal and, according to the Bible, everyone should "love their neighbors as themselves," was something the church supported. Yet when I attended my dad's church (Lutheran, Wisconsin Synod), they would not allow me to partake in communion because, although I was Lutheran, I was of the Missouri Synod. To me, this constituted excluding people because of differences. Was this then part of the "love your neighbor as yourself" idea? In grade school, I also remember studying about Native Americans. However, I remember studying stereotypical components of their culture, such as tepees, baskets, and canoes. I have since learned that these physical elements were parts of the cultures of certain American Indian groups, but they were by no means the most essential parts of them. So I wonder whether this was sufficient to instill in me the value of accepting differences!

With these differing impressions and attitudes, I was determined to find out for myself what to believe and think. My best friend was a good example of this. Kathryn is Canadian and English and practices the Moravian religion. Of course this religion was new to me and to my family since we had never been exposed to it. Immediately my father asked, "What kind of religion is that?" My mother, however, thought nothing of our differences and did not hesitate to let me spend free time with Kathryn and her family, which included going to church with them. To this day, if I go to a Catholic church rather than a Lutheran church, he says it is like not going to church at all.

Unfortunately, religion was not the only factor that had fallen prey to prejudice. Prejudice did not stop at our high school doors. The Native American students were shunned and looked down upon by many students. Charley, one Native American student, however, was seeing one of my good friends, and I had a conversation with him that I will never forget. He was on the verge of dropping out of high school, and I was trying to convince him not to. He asked me why he should try to do anything since, if he fails, the government would take care of him, just as it had taken care of his alcoholic father and grandfather. This angered me. I asked him if he wanted more out of life or if he just wanted to roll over and die and let the rest of the world pass him by. He knew the stereotypes others held against him and considered living up (or down) to their standards. I told him then everyone else would win and he would be the ultimate loser, proving everyone else was right. I do not know what became of Charley, but I think he did graduate from high school.

I do know that I learned several things from that conversation. Stereotypes can and do hurt. Charley had no positive role models, and he knew what others thought and expected from him. Because of this he considered becoming what everyone else was sure he would be—a poor, alcoholic, uneducated Indian. Also, maybe some governmental programs and policies do more harm than good. A weak person in Charley's shoes probably would have taken the easy way out and lived as his forefathers had, simply because it is the easiest thing to do. Yet maybe the policies the government has concerning Native Americans causes them to lose some of their dignity.

Charley, though, was not the only Native American I knew. My sister's (Donna's) best friend, Lydia, is also Native American. When we were younger, she would visit us often, and she is still the funniest person I have ever met. My mother, and the rest of us (excluding my stepfather), accepted her into our family as a sister, just as we did Kathryn. Her happy go lucky way of life and her refusal to fall prey to injustice was obvious.

Just recently I learned of a situation she and my sister experienced in grade school that proves that prejudice and racism also affected the educators at our school. One teacher in particular used to give Lydia a difficult time in class. Lydia was often singled out for punishment when a group of students was responsible. Noticing this, my sister made a rather rude comment and the teacher heard her. Both were sent to the principal's office and parents were called. My mother stood up for Donna and Lydia. Of course only those involved know the specifics of the story, but I suspect that both parties were guilty: Donna and Lydia of disrespect for a teacher; the teacher, of prejudice. Whatever the situation, I was proud to hear that my sister and my mother stood up for what they believed in.

Exchange students were another outlet for diversity in my high school, and I gained meaningful experiences from each of them. From Lydia, who was visiting from Mexico, I learned how difficult language barriers can be and how deeply someone can be hurt by another's insensitivity. Even though she was from another country and spoke a different language, she had still fallen prey to injustices. She had a very difficult time with English and was very naive. Some students took advantage of this and teased her. She broke down one day and cried during play practice and shared her feelings with me. She said it was hard for her to know who her real friends were and who just wanted to know her because she was the popular foreign exchange student. From this, I also realized how cruel people can be to others simply because of their differences. From Hiroko, I learned the different cultural aspects of Japan. I saw her struggle with the cultural aspects of Japan. I saw her struggle with the cultural differences of America and how they clashed with the culture of her native Japan. She did not want to go home to her family—she loved America and American culture so much. From this I could see the difficulties caused by assimilation and the mixing of cultures.

As a college student, I began working in various places and this increased my awareness of other cultures, races, and nationalities. For a while I worked for a Laotian family (whom some people called "gooks") who owned a restaurant. I must admit, I was a little intimidated by them since I knew little of their culture and language. When they spoke to each other, they spoke their native language, and it made me uncomfortable. I was also astounded by their work ethic and how generous they were. They worked around the clock and were always slipping me tens and twenties.

One day, though, the owner asked me about "the white powder." He told me how much he used and that maybe I should try it so I would not be tired. This frightened me, and I quit my job as soon as I could find another one. Even though I considered this to be a negative experience, I still realized the positive qualities of the family. The sons and daughters were also struggling with assimilation and, of course, the parents were trying to instill in them their culture rather than the culture of America. Later I learned that opium is an acceptable part of some Asian cultures. This also changed my feelings about this experience.

Not only did personal experiences with other races, religions, and cultures at work play a role in forming my attitudes, but so did college. About a year later, I took a class that had a major impact on me—Sociology 101. Every week we had a guest speaker of a different race or ethnic group. What I learned was eye opening. I applied much of this to my life and to my attitudes, putting myself in the shoes of those different from myself. I did this to try to understand others and their ways. What I learned made me become almost intolerant of ignorance and prejudice. For example, one summer I worked weeding ginseng as a second job. The woman in charge, Edna, was adamant in her claims of the Hmongs' deceit and trickery. She claimed they were ruining the market for ginseng and were adding other ingredients to their ginseng to get more money for less of the product. She said other things about them as well. I do not remember what I said to her after her "sermon against the Hmongs," but never again did she speak to me about her ideas concerning other groups of people—and I was glad.

During the school year, in college, I also worked at a pharmacy. My employer was very prejudiced against the Hmongs and was gossiping with several other employees one day when I came for work. Her claims against the Hmong ranged from "they eat dog meat" to a supposed incident in which a Hmong family planted a garden inside their apartment and ruined the new apartment. With the knowledge I gained from the sociology class I had taken, I explained to her how difficult the change in culture must be for the Hmongs and that this environment was completely foreign to them. It would take a while for them to become assimilated to the U.S. culture. From the look on her face, I could see she was disappointed in me. We never spoke about the Hmongs again.

In college, I also had many friends and acquaintances of various religions and nationalities. But in Stevens Point there still was not much diversity, and I do not recall having any friends of a different race. Of my friends and acquaintances, I can honestly say that I do not remember their religions and nationalities. After college though, I met and became friends with members of different races as well as different religions and nationalities—African Americans, Asians, several people of Spanish descent, and many people of various religions such as Catholic, Methodist, and Baptist.

In considering these experiences and being faced with the question of whether I would be willing to date (even marry) someone of another race, I would have to say I would have no problem with it. If I fell in love with someone of a different race and he made me happy, I would marry him. Even though I feel this way, I think some of my relatives, specifically my father and his side of the family, would have a difficult time with this. I think this is true because he grew up with prejudice and racism (as I can recall from comments made by his parents, my grandparents).

In reflecting on these experiences, I grew up with prejudice and racism. I think this has to do with the fear of the unknown. Since our area is populated with a majority of Caucasians of similar descent, many people had little opportunity to experience or learn of people different from themselves, which left many people ignorant.

Yet, if people fail to have experiences with other cultures, religions, and races, they have no opportunity to dispel the ideas of racism and prejudice that they may have learned at a very young age. Of course, this is only my opinion and perhaps my own ignorance and limited experience could account for this idea.

Because of my experiences and my education, I am thankful for my (few though they may be) experiences with members of various races, nationalities, and religions since they have left me with a fuller understanding and appreciation of others and their differences.

SOMETHING WENT WRONG

As I look back on my childhood I remember a few experiences that I had encountered with people of different racial backgrounds. The first experience that comes to mind is when I was in the third grade. On the fourth day of school, I remember hopping on the school bus and seeing two little Black boys and one Black girl sitting in the front seat. It was very unusual because in my town of three hundred, everyone seemed to be somehow related to the other; and if this was the situation, something went wrong along the way! The entire way to school, everyone talked quietly about the "two Black boys" and "the little Black girl who doesn't comb her hair" in the front seat.

At school the same thing occurred. Everyone avoided them and yet, behind their backs, talked about them. The girl and one of the Black boys were in my class and the other was in the class ahead of me. My sister and I felt bad for them so we went and talked to them. After some time they became our friends. Our teacher seemed to dislike colored people. I guess I shouldn't say that I knew that, but every day she yelled at them and locked them in a room. The boys became angry and on many occasions would hit her. The girl was very quiet and seldom spoke. Not too long after that they left the school and moved to Milwaukee.

When I was in the fifth grade, I was moved to a different school, where my class met up with one from another school to form one huge class. There I met a lot of new people, again like me. Everyone, for the most part, was White. When our class was split into two, I noticed a girl in my class who was unlike me. She was an Indian. She was very similar to the rest of us, except she had a tint to her skin, she dressed different, and she always wore her hair in braids. No one ever talked to her. Instead, everyone called her "little pow-wow girl" and many other names. I remember many days where she would sit in the corner and cry. After a few months she too had to leave our school and moved on.

From grade school to college, the only different people I ever encountered were the foreign exchange students. Throughout high school we learned about different cultures and races. We learned to treat them the same as we would treat anyone else. It was strange because so many students in our school would ignore or laugh at these foreign exchange students. When I entered college it was a dramatic change. Everywhere I looked, there were people of different races, nationalities, and religions. Walking to class I would often hear people behind me speaking a different language and laughing. At that point, I felt like I was the Black boy in grade school or that Indian girl in middle school. I felt out of place.

As time went on, I interacted with them and became good friends with many. I worked with Blacks, Chinese, Indians, and many others. I learned a great deal about their backgrounds and cultures. I was brought up to never judge people by their color or religion. I feel that I can learn so much by interacting with them. I can see how they differ from me and how their values and beliefs compare to mine. Even though I find interacting with people of different races, nationalities, and religions to be very beneficial to my growth, I still am around people who make stereotypical remarks and derogatory statements about people of different races, religions, and nationalities. Today I hear a lot of "Why don't you go back to your own country and leave us alone?" or "In America you speak our language or you don't belong here!"

There is one statement in my class readings that I fully agree with and that is that "racial and ethnic discrimination is the problem of Whites." I would definitely agree with that, because I experienced it as I was growing up. The two Black boys and the Indian girl never created the problems. It was us Whites. I don't think that Whites could accept other races or ethnic groups entering their "territory." I also agree that the media is playing a major role in correcting society and its prejudices. Also, I agree that discrimination affects human growth. I saw that in the Black family who moved to my town. They were affected by the way people were treating them.

However, there are a number of positive things that I see happening. In many ways, our society is changing and needs to change to create more of an "equal" society. I think, overall, we have come a long way in improving the discrimination and oppression in our society. Even though some still exists, we are on our way to a better, more equal world. I believe, personally, that we are all human. It doesn't matter what color we are—we all bleed red! We are all one!!

WE DROVE THE REDNECKS CRAZY

I grew up in a very small farming community in northern Iowa that was a high WASP area. My parents and grandparents were very well read people and never resorted to the use of racially oriented words. Not until about second or third grade did I start hearing the words "nigger," "spic," "greaser," "Jew," "Christ Killer," "Jap," "Chink," "Mackerel Snapper," and so forth. Being an inquisitive child, I asked at home and was told, "People who say those things are ignorant, just ignore them." Unfortunately, that did not help me much in preparing for the real world.

My first memory of active racial prejudice was church related. Our minister (Presbyterian) arranged a pulpit exchange with a Black minister from a city over a hundred miles away. We were going to their church for services and they, in turn, were coming to ours. There was really very little overt reaction to this idea. However, the night before we were to leave, someone slashed the tires, broke windows, and ripped out the engine wires on the church van. As a result, we never did go to the Black church. The perpetrators of these actions were never named either. I believe that I was about eleven or twelve at the time. All this made me wonder just exactly what could possibly be wrong with the idea of mingling with the Blacks and sharing our cultures.

The community was largely Protestant, with a few Catholics, one of whom was a very good friend of mine. I remember wondering just what exactly all the controversy was concerning the Catholics. The only difference between Mary Kaye and me was that she had to go to church Saturday mornings and she couldn't eat meat on Fridays. For some reason, the idea of not eating meat on Fridays was particularly upsetting to the other kids. They seemed to take it as a personal affront to have to eat macaroni and cheese instead of meat in their school lunches on Friday. As for me, I like fish so what the heck!

During my sophomore year of high school, we had the opportunity to have a German student attend our school for the year. Being of some German background myself (as, by the way, were most of the other members of the community), I found this a very interesting time. Tom was very intelligent and had a great sense of humor. Being better trained in the English language than the American students, he was laughed at for speaking properly! Since he was not familiar with our mannerisms and colloquialisms, he would often pull off a few verbal "boners," and be left wondering why everyone was laughing so hard. By the time he left our school (on his way to medical school, he'd already passed out of gymnasium, or the first college level in Germany), he was pretty much accepted by most of the students.

During my junior year of high school, our minister went on a pulpit exchange to New Zealand. When he returned, his family brought back a Maori student with them. Tom, as his name was also called, was very athletic and wonderfully handsome and his English accent didn't hurt either, especially since this was the time of the "British Invasion" that American teens of the time loved so well. He was a competent student but not as outstandingly intelligent as the other Tom, from Germany, had been. This Tom fit right in, even though he was a "foreigner" and was sought after by girls and boys alike.

The early 1970s was a time of acceptance, at least in the part of the country in which I lived. At college, I studied with, worked with, and spent leisure time with East Indians, American Indians, Blacks, Orientals, Hispanics, Catholics, Jews, Buddhists, and atheists. Four of us girls had an apartment together. Peggy was an American of Irish descent, Marta was from Bogota, Columbia, Noriko was from Tokyo, and I'm kind of a Heinz 57—English, Irish, Scottish, German, Danish, and probably a few other mixtures. There was nothing different about any of us. We were all girls, all interested in clothes, men, good grades, and where we were going in life. The fact that we weren't all from the same culture didn't bother us a bit. One of our best male friends was Tiny, a Black student from Des Moines. Tiny kind of destroyed the idea of stereotypes forever for me. He wasn't athletic, he could fall over his own feet, he was tone deaf, and he was extremely bright. So much for the dumb, athletic, dancing, musical Black man!

After leaving school and starting to work, I had a doctor who was Lebanese, one who was an East Indian (his father had been one of my psychology professors in college), and one doctor who was a native Hawaiian (but he was an American so what the heck!). I have worked for a Jewish private investigator (yes, he was kosher). In the same job, I worked assignments with a Black man. Bob was very nice and one of our best operatives. However, he was also a bit of a klutz. He didn't know one end of the football field, basketball court, or baseball diamond from the other and was even more tone deaf than Tiny! Surprise, surprise! We did quite a bit of work in St. Louis and did run into quite a bit of racism there regarding the Black man/White woman aspect. After the first few times it didn't bother us any more, but it certainly drove the rednecks crazy!

This all appears to be going nowhere fast so I'm going to attempt a summation at this time. My personal feelings are that no matter what color, religion, or society a person is from, everyone has the right to express their own ideas, practice their own religion, cultural beliefs, and customs, and attempt to improve their lot in life. This is, perhaps, an unfashionable view. This is not necessarily to say that I am a screaming liberal. Far from it. I am very definitely opposed to the Jamaican drug traffickers, the Cuban drug traffickers, and any other group involved in drug dealing. I am also highly opposed to the illegal aliens. I am not opposed to them as a people, I am opposed to them because of what they do; but I am equally against the White drug dealers, pimps, murderers, and perverts (realizing, of course, that pervasion is in the eye of the beholder.) I am not against Mexicans as a whole. I have several very good Hispanic friends. However, they and their families took the time to study and become active and productive American citizens. This goes for all races. I feel that if any person is willing to take the time to achieve citizenship, more power to them. (By the way, I seriously doubt that many, if any, good "Americans" could successfully complete the citizenship exams.) After all, there was a time when the Irish were looked down upon in America and since I have several Irish ancestors, I'm certainly not about to cast any stones. As far as I'm concerned, a person is a person. As for other cultures, we'd probably still be trying to figure out how to create fire or invent the wheel if not for the fact that throughout history, cultures have constantly traded ideas.

Unfortunately, I am only one person and feelings of ethnocentrism are the norm in our country. We may cry out against apartheid—but are we really any better? Once America was proud of its title of "the melting pot of the world." Perhaps we would all be better off if we would regain our pride in this title and learn to live together and pull together as a country instead of trying to prove that the only "good" American is descended from the Lowells or the Cabots.

HE TREATS ME LIKE A QUEEN

In life I was taught that it was okay to talk to people who happened to look different from me, though, it was not encouraged to be very friendly with people who were of another race. I believe this was because of the variety of stereotypes that society had developed. In the following, I will talk about what it was like rooming with two different people of two different races and a relationship with a significant other of another race and friends who have a different religion.

Early in my life I was taught to make friends with people who are basically like me. As early as kindergarten, I was sent to a Catholic grade school. This was a very small school. My eighth grade class graduated with thirteen students. I remember many times walking home from school and I was made fun of because of the uniform that I was required to wear. This fact helped me to understand what it would be like to be the only person of another race because I, too, was different. At first it was hard taking all the comments, but then I realized that this was who I was and that could not be changed.

When I was in high school, I heard some different phrases that upset me. I remember phrases referring to the Blacks, Asians, Caucasians, Native Americans, and people of mixed parenting. Many times the Blacks were called "chocolate drops," "nigger," "spear chucker," "porch monkey," "darkie," and "boy/house boy." Secondly, at times the Asians were called such names as "chink," "Jap," and "slope." Plus, when people referred to all Asians they were called "dogs." Thirdly, the Caucasians also were called names. These included names such as "whitey," "red-neck," "ghost," and "pale face." Next, the Native Americans were called "spear chucker" and "Tonto." Lastly, sons and daughters of mixed races were called "Neopolitan." The thought of people being called these different names upsets me because it makes me realize why so many people have a low self-esteem. The fact that people are calling others names to intentionally hurt them makes me wonder what kind of world we are actually living in.

Since I went to college, I roomed with three different people. One was Black, another was White, and the remaining one was Asian. The three different roommates were interesting to live with. I found that the Black and the Asian roommates were the easiest to live with. We had our differences at times, but they were open minded so we could talk things out. I feel that my relationships were stronger among my roommates of another race.

I invited people from other cultural backgrounds into my home. I never limited my friendships on the basis of race or religion. I feel if people want to know about my race or religion they should ask and I would be happy to inform them.

Currently, I am dating a young man who happens to be of another race. Yes, if he ever asked me to marry him I would say yes in an instant. I would not have to give it a second thought. The only negative aspect is the fact that our children will be of two different races. This can cause some problems because our children may have identity problems. However, this is something that can be resolved.

He is a wonderful guy and treats me like a queen. He is gentle with me. Also, I never have to worry about him hurting me. He does not have it in him to hurt anybody. This is the best relationship I have ever been involved in. Plus, I would encourage anyone to have an interracial relationship. I found that we have so much in common and that I enjoy his company so much. I think if people can look past the skin color, they will see people for whom they really are.

SUMMARY

We can conclude from these essays that general education does help lessen prejudice and that the benefits from education are transmitted from one generation to the next. Thus, if the parents are well-educated, ethnically cosmopolitan people, their children are also likely to be ethnically cosmopolitan.

But we also find considerable evidence to show that persons with more formal education did not necessarily express more tolerant attitudes toward minority groups. However, as their education helped them acquire jobs that moved them to various cities in the country and to various parts of the world, this helped to break the provincialism that they previously had. As a result, they began to appreciate diversity and also encouraged their children to be more tolerant of others.

Thus, the acceptance of diversity by persons with higher education may not be due to their educational levels. The differences in education may be correlated with other forces that help to reduce prejudice such as the chances of equal-to-equal interaction with diverse populations that their education enhances. In other cases, it might be the greater exposure to the world that the well educated have through employment opportunities. Overall the essays show us that education is a liberating tool to the recipients and can help dampen prejudices.

6

Coming to America

For years, America has been a haven for immigrants from various parts of the world. Each immigrant comes to this country with a different life story and a different background. For many, America is the land where their childhood dreams can be fulfilled. Yet, each stream of immigrants encounters difficulties fitting into American society. The need to blend in has become even more difficult for recent immigrants, most of whom originate from non-European countries. Be that as it may, these difficulties are seen by immigrants not as stumbling blocks but as obstacles to be overcome in the pursuit of their dreams.

The stories of the recent immigrants in this chapter show us that the cultural and ethnic problems that America is confronted with are not unique to this country but that every country has its own social problems to overcome. Such problems may be religious, as in the case of Iran, or ethnic, as in the case of Malaysia. What is different, the stories of the immigrants tell us, is how each country responds to diversity and the opportunities that are made avaliable to persons of diverse ethnic and racial groups. It would seem that despite the sociocultural problems that America faces, America still provides better opportunities for the advancement of its minority groups than do other countries. This may explain why America continues to be a magnet for many in the world.

The essayists also testify that worldviews, social institutions, and artifacts are the vehicles through which each culture socializes its young to embrace established attitudes of race, ethnicity, and religion. They do this in order to perpetuate a sense of peoplehood—a "we-them" mentality.

I AM AMERICAN

In this essay I will reflect on being a minority in the United States of America. I will explain how it feels to grow up in an all-White society as a minority. Also, I will reflect on how I do not look at myself as a minority in America.

When I was a baby, I was adopted from Seoul, South Korea. My parents are Caucasian and my sister and I are both Korean. My sister and I are the only Koreans in our immediate and extended family. We both have grown up as American children and not as Korean children. We may look the part, but we do not act the part. Even though we grew up American, many people assume that we are Korean all the way through. Throughout my childhood, I have been teased about my nationality. In elementary school, boys, as well as girls, would tease us about our eyes, nose, and skin color. They would say our noses are flat because we ran into the wall when we were children. Also, they teased us for not seeing as well as Whites because our eyes are slanted. Children can really be mean! I will always remember what my dad told my sister and me when we were little. If other children were being mean or teasing us about being Korean, my dad told us that we had the right to punch them for teasing us. If we got detention for it, it would not bother him in any way. There was only one other Korean girl in my elementary school. The three of us were the only race other than Caucasian.

My elementary school principal was very fond of my sister, the other Korean girl, and me. The reason for this is that my principal had adopted a Korean girl. Many times, throughout my elementary years, I was called down to the principal's office. I was not in trouble. He just wanted to talk with us or give us a present. In this case, we were favored for being the minority in the school.

Throughout my life so far, I have always been in the minority. I never thought of myself that way though. My friends and family are all Caucasians. I grew up in an all-White community. I was never discriminated against for being Korean. I grew up in the same town my whole life so everyone knew who I was. I do remember getting a lot of attention as a child. Everywhere we went, when my sister and I were little, everyone thought that we were so cute. I know that a lot of it had to do with us being Korean children and not Caucasian children. It was not a common thing to have adopted children from another country at that time.

My parents raised my sister and me as American children. We were not given any special treatment by my parents, or anyone else, because of our race. I know my parents, relatives, and friends think of me as an American and not a Korean. My race has never been an issue we discussed. A lot of the time when we run into people who say something about my race, my friends would say, "Are you Korean? We haven't even noticed." This is a big joke that we all have with each other. All my friends see me as one of them and not someone from another country. I have some friends who are also Korean or are of Asian descent. Many of them grew up like me and think of themselves as American.

I believe that I have a very open mind when it comes to people of a different race, color, or religion. I know that my parents and relatives do not share this open-mindedness with me. I know my parents have a personal bias against Blacks. I personally do not understand this bias. I am not "White," and they do not treat me with a bias. I personally have never dated a Korean guy. It is not that I have not had the opportunity, I just decided not to. My boyfriend right now is Caucasian. All my boyfriends in the past have been Caucasian. All my relationships have been what people call "interracial dating." I never think of myself as on an interracial date. I know that I will marry into an interracial marriage. I also know that my boyfriend does not have a problem with me being Korean. He sees me for who I am and not my skin color. As I said before, I see myself as American, and not Korean, in the whole sense.

Throughout my life I know that I will come in contact with people who will not accept me for who I am. I figure that it is their loss and not mine. I hope that someday the world will open its eyes and see everyone for whom they are and not what color they are.

THEY HARDLY CALL ON ME

I consider myself very lucky because I have had the opportunity to live in several countries with different racial groups and cultural backgrounds from the time I was in grade school up until college. I had been exposed to cultural diversities at a very early age. Most important was my parents' influence on me. The way that I was brought up had a great impact on my whole perspective about life and people in general.

I was born in Laos. My ethnic background is Hmong. At a very early age, I had already been exposed to all kinds of people. For example, there are other ethnic groups such as Chinese, Vietnamese, and Cambodians living in Laos, too. I grew up living with all these ethnic groups. When I was a kid, the idea of stereotypes never occurred to me. My parents taught me that God makes all kinds of people and that everyone is unique and different.

In Laos, it is very common for people to walk into anyone's house and ask for a place to stay for the night, especially if they are from out of town. My parents would welcome strangers to stay overnight, including the homeless, monks, the insane, and blind people as well. Occasionally, there were people who practiced black magic or Voodoo who came to spend the night in our house. They would stay up and meditate all night long. These people didn't want to sleep or stay in the guest room. They usually preferred to stay in the kitchen or outside on the balcony. The strangest thing was that all these strange people always left our house before sunrise. They never stayed long enough for breakfast, nor did they want anything to eat for dinner, even when we offered them some food. Until now, I never really understood why, because I didn't have the chance to ask my parents. They both passed away when I was very young. However, they taught me the most important thing in life—if you give someone onefold, you will receive threefold in return.

When I was a kid, racism and stereotyping were never mentioned in my family. Once in a while, when my parents were not home, my neighbors would tell me that we shouldn't let those crazy strange people into our house because they could kill us. A lot of our neighbors didn't welcome any strangers into their houses. Our house was not so easy to find, but somehow these people always found their way. Perhaps it was because no one in town welcomed them. Another reason might be that a lot of strangers knew my father. Strangers always told me that my father was the kindest and nicest man in town. My parents always encouraged my brothers and me to think positively about people. They said, "If you want to help someone, you should help the person with an open mind and without questioning." We never asked any of these people about their religious, racial, or ethnic backgrounds.

All these ideas about racism and stereotypes didn't occur to me until l was twelve years old. When my brother and I escaped from the Communists in Laos to Thailand, we were forced to pay a large sum of money to the Thai government. Still, they took us to stay in the concentration camp. They thought Hmong people were filthy and inferior to people in Thailand.

Worse yet, when I came to the United States, everything here was new to me. I didn't speak English at the time. It didn't matter what people said to me, because I couldn't understand. I thought everyone was so kind and nice. I have had some good and bad experiences with Americans. Since I went to school (eighth grade through high school), I encountered many problems with some of my classmates who were extremely racist. They constantly picked on me. They would call me names, such as "stupid Oriental." Some of my teachers would send those students who treated me badly in class to the principal's office, but as for other teachers, they just laughed when someone made fun of me or another student. However, I also had many American friends who were loyal, honest, nice, and cared deeply about me.

Many of the discrimination problems that continued throughout high school were from some of the same people who went to school with me in eighth grade. Well, back then I still had a lot of self-esteem, pride, and dignity. The point is, I hadn't done anything wrong, why should I be afraid. I wasn't afraid of anyone. If they cursed me out, made fun of me, or called me names, I would say whatever they said to me back. I told them that I was not the problem. Whatever they called me, that is what they were, so they stopped picking on me. There were a few people who actually apologized to me because they realized that they only made fools out of themselves.

In college I think students are more accepting of ethnic diversity. A lot of the problems that I am facing in college have to do with the professors. For example, if I get an A on the test, they think that I cheated; and if I get a C, they think that I'm not smart enough to take the class. For example, one semester in one of my courses, I received A's on all my term papers and the professor asked me if anyone was helping me write my papers. She was implying that I couldn't have made A's without someone helping me. I told the professor that even though my English was not perfect, "I'm here to learn and I got A's because I spent a lot of time revising my papers." Normally I am very talkative, but now I'm kind of hesitating to participate in class because I had some bad experiences with some of the professors at Normal College. They hardly call on me, even when I raise my hand first. It doesn't mean that I should quit participating, but I just don't feel comfortable participating in class anymore.

When it comes to interracial marriage, Hmong people are least likely to accept it. A lot of the stereotypes that I heard are: interracial marriages don't last; two out of three interracial marriages end up in divorce; it never lasts more than three years; the guy will divorce you after having one kid; the in-laws will force their son to marry someone from their own race; children from interracial marriages are no good; and nice girls shouldn't marry into another race. Anyone married to another race is considered a disgrace to his or her family and its people. Since my parents passed away a long time ago, I was brought up by my three brothers. I thought they were very open minded. They didn't mind when I dated someone besides Hmong boys. They always told me that it didn't matter who I married, as long as that person loves and respects me. I never thought they would mind if I happened to marry someone outside of my race, because they never mentioned that I should not marry someone of another race. However, when they found out that I was engaged to a Chinese guy, they were furious. I was so shocked when they taught me one thing and expected the opposite. Anyway, I went ahead and got married. Some of my relatives and cousins refused to come to my wedding. They said that what I did was a disgrace to them. Many of them no longer want to have any contact with me. It is sad, but I can't change their minds.

I think racism is ethnocentric and stereotyping is attitudinal. People judge others based on what they believe. Some information might be true but it doesn't apply to everyone. I think people should try to separate fact from fiction. Most important, community, church, family, and peers have a great influence on our attitudes toward people, and about who we are as individuals.

AMERICA, THE EQUAL PROVIDER

The impressions and attitudes that my family instilled in me toward the issues of race and religion were very positive, meaning that I was taught to look at different racial or religious groups with respect and the understanding that all people are God-created individuals regardless of their race or religion. However, the impressions and attitudes toward people of different races and ethnic groups that school instilled in me were different. I was taught that Islam was superior to any other religion, and that every religion other than Islam was imperfect. Other institutions, such as the community or society as a whole, were hostile toward people from other religions. However, race was not an issue in Iran because Iran is a unicultural country and everyone is considered a Persian. My experience as a Christian was quite negative, because I was always treated like a second-class person. I was looked at differently in schools, in the army, and in different institutions within the society. I think it was at the age of fourteen or fifteen that I realized how divided our country was, based on the issue of religion. I think that the gap between Islam and other religions in Iran is a lot larger than the gap between Blacks and Whites in America. Unlike Iran, at least here in America the government recognizes the rights of minorities, and puts these rights into law in order to enforce them.

When I came to America and started college, I had the chance to meet students from every part of the world. Unlike some countries, America is an equal provider of education, and everyone regardless of race, religion, color, or national origin can attend school if they wish to. Living in a diverse society like America, and attending college, gave me the chance to sit in classrooms full of foreign students who chose American schools for an advanced education. Basically, classrooms were the only opportunities I had to meet people of other races or religions.

I very much like to meet people of other racial or religious groups. People of different racial and religious groups have been to my house as guests many times. I also have them as neighbors, schoolmates, and work colleagues. They're basically from different cultures with different social behaviors. They believe in different religions, and they have different ways of defining social norms. I will have no problem dating or marrying someone of a different race or ethnic background.

I BECAME PREJUDICED

I was born in Russia, raised in Africa for six years, and have been in the United States ever since. I have lived in Texas and in Kansas. I moved to Olathe, Kansas, my sophomore year, and after going to school there, I became prejudiced.

My parents did not bring me up to be prejudiced or racist. They always told me, "You are a minority as far as gender and race are concerned, so don't let anyone try to take your education from you." As far as schools go, when I lived in Africa, I was attending an African school. In Texas, I attended a multicultural school, and I did not see any prejudice in either of those schools. Then when I moved back to Kansas, I noticed prejudice toward me, and I became prejudiced.

One noteworthy experience that I had with another race was when I was walking to class one day and accidentally bumped into someone. I turned around to apologize to him and he called me a "damn nigger." I then dropped my books and pushed him down as hard as I could. He was getting up to hit me, he hit me once, and then I threw one of my books at him. We were then escorted to the principal's office by an angry teacher. My principal was a Cuban female who gave me two days in-school suspension. The guy, who claimed to be a KKK, got one day out-of-school suspension and two days in-school suspension. This continued through the end of the school year. My girl friends got involved to support me. A few boys got involved in support of the boy who hit me, claiming to be KKK's. They walked down the hallway calling my friends and me "niggers," and two Caucasian girls who hung around my friends and me "nigger lovers." My friends and I walked down the hallway calling them "honkey," "crackers," and "White trash." Although I was a junior, I felt I only reacted that way because I was not used to prejudice being directed at me face to face.

This has been my second semester in college, and taking this class, I get to hear what some people of other races think of my race. In Texas we lived in a multicultural area. I had all kinds of neighbors. My family never had any problems with these neighbors, especially when we lived by the Russians. They invited my family to eat dinner with them, and vice versa. In Affluent City, I only had Caucasian neighbors. They did not speak to us, and we did not speak to them. Now we live in a new neighborhood in Affluent County, where one of our neighbors is Indian. They are the only ones who associate with my family, and they are the only ones we associate with.

After living in many different places and presently living in a predominantly White area, I have become prejudiced. I feel a person is prejudiced because of their community. I am speaking for myself, and that's how I ended up having a little prejudice in me. After facing prejudice, I don't think I will ever marry someone of another race. If I do, it will have to be another minority, because I feel that he has gone through the same thing, or worse.

THE CONTRADICTION

I was brought up in a family who taught me to have a good attitude toward other people and respect them regardless of their race, sex, age, or religion. Back in my country, during my school years or in other institutions, I never heard of any stereotyping, racism, or religious problems.

When I came to the United States at the age of thirteen, I heard of many problems in the public or the media relating to sex, age, and racial discrimination. I even experienced it myself. The experiences that I mostly faced were racial discrimination because of my color. Whether I was in school or in public, some Americans would call me names, beat me up, or throw things at me. They even accused us of taking their country and jobs away from them and said that we were lazy. However, I still don't understand the contradictions in them—when we worked they said that we took their jobs away; and when we didn't work, they said we were lazy. Sometimes I wondered what it was they really wanted from us.

Since I came to college, I am surprised that I have not as yet faced any racial problems. Maybe it is because people have more knowledge about racism or maybe the racism is there but people keep it to themselves. I have been able to make friends with people of other races, nationalities, and religions. We've had people from different nationalities, races, and religions as our guests. Some of these people were our relatives, and some were our friends who came to visit my family once in a while in the summer. My neighbors are all American, but I don't mind having people of other races or nationalities as my neighbors. I have them as my schoolmates and as my fellow employees. I don't mind dating (even marrying) someone of another race if I find the right person. My viewpoint is that the reason Asians, Blacks, Chicanos, and others have not become assimilated and continue to be objects of discrimination is because of their readily recognizable physical characteristics.

THE OUTSIDER

I do not consider myself to be racist or closed minded. I have to give my immediate family credit for my nonjudgmental upbringing. Ever since I found out that I was adopted, my family has never taught me to judge people on the basis of race, color, or nationality.

On the other hand, my extended family treated me as an outsider. My cousins did not want to play with me because I looked and acted differently from them. They were very apprehensive and could not understand why my family adopted me. Eventually, they learned to accept me.

School was pretty much the same way. I was always one of the few minorities in the school. I was the first contact with a "foreigner" for most children from kindergarten through senior year . I admit that I felt out of place and that I had to prove myself to all the children. Also I was probably the most accepted of the minorities.

For instance, from kindergarten through sixth grade, there was a family from India. They were not accepted into the community because of their customs. Actually, the neighborhood was cruel to them. Hardly anyone would be their friends.

I remember that the schoolchildren were especially mean to Rashna and Anurage. They would tease them because of their body odor. Since I was their friend, I was the one who had to tell them that in the United States we take more showers and wash our clothes more. It was not that they did not do those things, but, they explained, it was from their diet. I felt sorry for them. Today they are back in India where they feel more welcome.

Another friend of mine named Collette had a tough time with the boys. Collette was also adopted by a Caucasian family. She was the only African American student.

Collette liked the White guys, but they did not like her back. They usually ended up liking me, because I was lighter skinned than her. I asked her why she did not go out with guys of her own race. Her answer was that she did not feel like she fit in with them and none of them liked her. I understood her because that is how it is with me.

There were a couple of guys whom I went out with until I found out why they were interested in me. Their rationale was that Asian girls are exotic, passive, and caretakers. They wanted me to be like a "doll." Little did they know that I do not fit the typical stereotype.

To this day, I do not have a problem with dating or marrying a man of a different nationality from me. My brother married a Mexican woman, and she has been welcomed into the family with open arms. Other members of the family have married Native Americans, African Americans, and Europeans.

In conclusion, I consider myself to be very open minded toward all cultures. I strongly believe that no matter what color, race, or sexual identity anyone is, we all are human beings with unique characteristics. That is what makes us individuals. I really am glad that my family never taught me to judge people based on their physical qualities.

IS THIS FREEDOM?

I am a Malaysian, and I was living in my own country during my childhood socialization. Malaysia is a multiracial society with three different religions and races. However, the most powerful race and the majority of the population are Malays. The second most populous group is Chinese with 33% of the population, followed by the Indians with 15%. Therefore, the political system and government is under the control of the Malays. Even though the constitution proclaims freedom of religion and equality for all races, there are restrictive laws that prohibit criticizing the ruling government or leaders. Thus, freedom of speech is not practiced.

I studied in *mandarin* in primary school for six years. At that time, I didn't have the opportunity to mix with Malays or Indians because all of the students were Chinese, and we were educated in Chinese. I didn't even realize the importance of racial and religious differences. Not until I stepped into secondary school did I begin to know a little more about politics, and racial and religious problems. In fact, there is unequal educational opportunity in Malaysia. The universities, or higher education, are mostly offered to the *bumiputra* Malays, and if you plan to compete with them to further your education, you must excel. That is why a lot of Chinese students plan to go overseas for their higher education. In other words, if you are a Malay, you can do anything you want and there is freedom of choice, but that is not the case for Chinese or Indians. Even though a small number of Chinese are eligible and fortunate enough to enter the universities, they have no choice in the career they pursue since this is chosen for them by the authorities.

Is this freedom? Freedom of choice? Free will? I think not. Instead, every aspect of life such as education, politics, and economics is determined and controlled. There is no such thing as freedom in my country.

I still remember when I was working in a shopping complex while waiting for my MCE (Malaysian Certificate of Education) results, a final grade of high school. I met and knew some of the Malay staff who were also waiting for their grades. They told me that to enter the universities is not tough, that it is easy for Malays. In other words, they did not need good grades to apply to the well-known universities. They discussed a lot of racial and religious problems with me and felt sorry that the same qualifications are not offered to other minorities, like Chinese and Indians.

When I was nineteen years old, I started a new life in the United States. I had traveled a long distance from my hometown to further my education at MCC. In my opinion, the only thing that is different from my country is the real freedom given in the United States to everyone without discrimination against people on the basis of color, religion, or national origin. I have been here for more than one year, and I have come to know some of my friends from Africa, Pakistan, Hong Kong, Taiwan, and even my fellow Americans. In fact, America is the best society where one can get to know and mix with people from different nationalities and races. However, discrimination should be eliminated, especially in this technologically advanced world. It remains as one of the social problems that can affect a person's life including job, activities, and behavior.

I don't really mind dating or even marrying someone of another race. Just because the color of a person's skin, religion, or nationality are different does not mean that that person should be discriminated against. In other words, I will be glad to have friends, neighbors, schoolmates, and fellow employees of different backgrounds, nationalities, races, and religions. In fact, some of the religions and races prohibit people from marrying people of other groups. I think that those social diseases should be eliminated and everyone should be able to share our similar inborn human rights.

A CITY OF DIFFERENT CULTURES

I did not see any differences in people when I was young. To me, we are all human beings, only we have different skin color. Inside of us, we are the same; we are people who have brains, organs, arms, and legs. The fact that I think this way is probably because I have been exposed to the West and East since I was little.

My nationality is Chinese. I was born in the United States, and my family moved back to Hong Kong when I was five years of age. Hong Kong is an international city. It is a popular vacation retreat. We have people from all over the world with different cultures. Hong Kongers are very open minded. I attended a school in Hong Kong where everyone was Chinese. By the time we moved to the United States, I went to public schools. The students were predominantly White. Occasionally you would see Black students and a few Chinese students. All the students got along great. Other students did not look down on us or the Blacks. Chinese students usually did well in school, and the Blacks were from good families. For that reason, other students had no reason to look down on the minorities. In addition to the above, most of the students from my school came from upper-middle-class families. I suppose most of the parents did not teach their children to be prejudiced.

My friends can be any color as long as they treat me nice and don't take advantage of me when I need them. I am only prejudiced against people who are rude and don't behave themselves.

As to whether I will marry someone of another race, one side of me tells me that if I really find someone whom I like very much, I will get married no matter what her skin color is. But the other side says interracial marriage will not work for me. I have seen interracial marriages work for some couples, but the majority of them do not work. It is hard to say. Finding someone who is compatible with yourself is not easy any more. People are more independent now than before.

A CHANGE OF MIND

I have had many different kinds of experiences with people of different ethnic groups. My fiance is White while I am mixed. We have had to put up with a lot of prejudice all around. He has adapted real well to the color differences, but I still wonder if I made the right decision when I got involved with someone of a different race. Because he is my fiance, I attend his church, which is all White. There are many racially biased people at the church, and I really don't know how to tell him I feel uncomfortable at the church. I am faced with many stereotypes at this church, simply because I am a person of color.

I come from Guyana. When I came to this country, I was not prejudiced in any way but due to the different circumstances that I have encountered with the opposite race—White—I do find myself somewhat racially inclined. What color you are, in this country, dictates your life chances. My mom cannot understand why I have changed so dramatically, but she has not been in the situations that I have been in.

SUMMARY

These essays demonstrate that in every country, the litmus test of difference in ethnicity, race, tribe, or religion is whether it is socially significant. That is, whether it affects interpersonal or intergroup interaction. The relevant issues then are whether race, or ethnicity, or tribe, or religion cause awe, anger, attraction, or repulsion and whether these differences are the basis of economic stratification, political power conflict, and role allocation. In other words, does ethnicity, race, and religion determine one's social status, prescribe and proscribe one's roles and role expectations in the social structure of a country?

In our essayists' countries of origin, just like in the United States, the answer to these questions is a resounding yes! In these countries, ethnocentrism and xenophobia, as aspects of racial, ethnic, and religious relations, result in the persecution and exile of numerous people of different minority, racial, religious, and ethnic backgrounds. In fact some of the essayists are in the United States as refugees from such catastrophes.

The essayists came to America because America has so long been the asylum for the oppressed and persecuted—and has done itself and the world so much good thereby—that any harassment of an immigrant offends something in the American soul. To the essayists, America is a welcoming country. That is why some of the essayists are disillusioned when they are confronted with prejudice and discrimination at school and at the workplace.

7

Something Old, Something New

A review of the essays shows that three social institutions play an important role in shaping the worldview of children, especially as it affects their relationships to diverse groups. These institutions are the family, peer groups, and the workplace. Of these, the family is the most important social institution, especially in the formative years of the child. The family is the first agent of socialization, and it is through the family unit that society's attitudes, beliefs, and behavioral expectations are introduced to the child. It is also in the formative years that a child begins the transition from egocentrism to sociocentrism.

Next to the family in importance to a child's socialization process and development is his or her peer group. This peer group influence can occur either at the neighborhood level as the child interacts with other children in the neighborhood and learns through role playing or in a more formal setting such as occurs in school. School, and the educational system in general, provides an acculturation medium where children are taught both cognitive and social skills. The essays show that school can be a liberating experience and a harbinger to racial openness.

The third agent of socialization is the workplace. The workplace provides a vital social environment for people to interact and to learn from each other. Unlike the family and peer group, however, the workplace plays a role in the lives of people after they have reached adulthood and therefore its impact in changing racial, ethnic, and religious stereotypes and attitudes is limited. Nevertheless, the workplace is unique in that it provides an opportunity for people to interact on an individual, and sometimes, equal footing. Since the objective of all workers is to ensure that the organization achieves its goals, personal differences and prejudices may be suppressed for the good of the organization. We discuss below how each of these social institutions affect a person's development and perceptions of diversity.

THE FAMILY AS A SOCIALIZING AGENT

Previous research on the role of the family in the socialization process of children, such as that by Morris (1981), found that even when parents encourage their children to interact with people of a different race, they usually shy away. This, she concluded, was due to "stranger anxiety," the belief that children naturally fear or have anxiety toward anything strange or different. This instinctive behavior of children, some bio-socio-psycho-determinists argue, helps to explain the development of prejudice even from infancy.

This explanation is, however, inadequate. Our view is that children are not only afraid of people of a different race, but rather, they are afraid of anybody and anything exotic (not pertaining to their significant others, in this case parents), because as they go through infantilization, children inevitably bond with their parents, and develop an indispensable dependency for survival. The survival instinct bonds them to the significant other so much so that they are afraid of strangers, including those of their parents' race or ethnicity. Children do not choose and pick who they are afraid of, like adult bigots do.

As the essayists testify, children, especially after five years of age, begin to outgrow the survival bonding instinct and strike out. They tend to reach out to others regardless of race and ethnicity. As children become more interested in understanding various social situations, the stereotypes or ideals they learned at home begin to either gain more, or lose, legitimacy. For instance, if their parents are prejudiced, the children may choose to clandestinely experience the prohibited fruit by befriending those that their parents warn them not to associate with. If these exploratory interactions were positive and continued over a long time, the curious child may begin to accept people of other races at the risk of losing favor with his or her parents.

Of course, the opportunity for a child to interact with people of other racial and ethnic groups was grievous for many of the essayists, especially those who did not travel abroad and those who lived in segregated neighborhoods. For those families who lived in segregated neighborhoods, this social distance continued even when families of a different race or ethnicity moved into the neighborhood. That ethnically or racially diverse families were physically located in the neighborhood did not necessarily guarantee contact between majority and minority children because some parents kept vigilance against contact between their children and *personae non grata* in the neighborhood. In fact, some White families fled their neighborhoods and moved into new neighborhoods to join their own kind in order to keep a safe distance from intruders and to protect their children from contact with minority groups.

For those children whose parents did not flee the neighborhood, these different families provided the social laboratories where the studious children tested their parents' race theories by defiantly playing with the *personae non grata* children. Thus, they were able to gather empirical data that they then used to reach their own conclusions about the different ethnic and racial groups. In many cases, these experiments disproved the prejudices of parents. As a result, the children were able to develop healthier racial attitudes than those of their parents.

However, increased contact between minority and majority groups is not sufficient in and of itself to dispel racial prejudices. A review of the essays indicate that in order for healthy racial attitudes to develop, contact between groups must be long and sustained. At a person-to-person level, increased contact with the prohibited child increased the restrained child's curiosity and friendship to people of the *personae non grata* group. This type of relationship leads to a distinction on the individual-difference level rather than on the group-stereotype level and goes to show that in order to counteract ethnic stereotypes, close, firsthand knowledge is required.

The accounts also show that increased contact between individuals of different racial or ethnic background enhances understanding and reduces prejudice only when the contact is motivated by genuine mutual human curiosity and inherent volunteerism. A person with no contact with other groups would gain no new information other than secondhand reports, which would usually tend to uphold the group stereotype or a biased cop-out "anchoring effect" that parents use as a prohibition mechanism to deter their children from contact with "those people." Simply put, children who have never had the chance early in life to interact with other races instinctively develop psychological and sociological anxiety and fear toward those who are different from them. Those essayists who grew up in small Midwestern towns, and who had little or no contact with minority groups, held derogatory attitudes and strong stereotypes of these groups. These attitudes and stereotypes were usually enhanced by socializing agents in their community.

By contrast, essayists who had increased racial exposure and contacts had a more positive attitude and a greater acceptance of minority groups. Children from mixed neighborhoods, well-traveled families, and interracial churches and schools had a higher preference for those of another race or ethnicity than children from segregated institutions. Whether they have had fistfights with each other or not, most essayists who had contact with *personae non grata* reported positive attitudes toward them. Overall, we found that there is an intergenerational gap between children and their parents with regard to openness and acceptance of diversity. Most of the students reportedly held more positive attitudes toward minority groups than did their parents. This may be due to the greater opportunity that these students now have to interact with people of diverse backgrounds, an opportunity that their parents did not have because of segregation laws. Among minority essayists, interracial institutions also increased self-esteem and own-race preference because such institutions gave them a chance to encounter on the same ground, compete on equal terms, and rise or fall on equal footing with children from White families.

The family, then, is an arena for early childhood development and a continued source of support for, and maintenance of, ethnic and race-based attitudes. Parents instill these values through explicit communication in instruction and child-rearing behaviors, by controlling intergroup interaction, and by establishing a lifestyle that influences the selection of their children's friends and playmates.

PEER GROUPS AS SOCIALIZING AGENTS

By the time children reach the age of eight, and as their social skills improve, they begin to associate and play with their peer group. Indeed, the peer group becomes so increasingly important that their lives begin to focus around the school and activities with friends. Thus, in addition to the family, children begin to be sensitive to the racial attitudes and beliefs of their peers.

As they grow older, children begin to cross-check the information they were given at home about diverse groups with those of their peers and their own experiences. If the child's peers hold opinions similar to what the child learned at home, then this gives validity to the views learned. Alternatively, children who are unable to validate their experience with what they learned at home may discard these opinions and trust their own experience.

Children's peers constituted the first agent of socialization the essayists actively chose. Through interacting with peers of a different background, the essayists learned about race, ethnicity, and religious matters in a nondeliberative and nonauthoritarian, participative manner. School and college mainly functioned as arenas, where the essayists met and interacted with peers of a different racial, ethnic, or religious background, in many cases for the first time. Some essayists described activities, episodes, and encounters in which they interacted or collaborated with others of different racial, ethnic, and national backgrounds. Such activities gave them the chance to walk, talk, and lunch together informally, and also enabled them to see each other as humans who aspire for the same things in life.

Through these activities, the essayists were able to make up their own minds about "the other race." Some even had the chance to cast out the stereotypes that they had brought with them from home. Others, unfortunately, just confirmed their "anchoring effects" and went on to full-blown prejudice. Through these away-from-home interactivities with people from diverse backgrounds, most essayists realized the importance of looking beyond skin color or ethnic costume in order to understand others. However, we also found examples that even though interaction and integration in schools, colleges, work, and play helped the essayists become aware of racial differences, for some, doing so did not always assure the unlearning of deep-seated racial biases acquired through the years of a monolithic and assimilationist policy, parents, and religion.

Many essayists related their educational experience in terms of how much interaction they had with children and teachers of a different racial or ethnic background. Some who had not had enough racial interaction, had bad experiences, or acquired information about other ethnic and racial groups indirectly confirm that early segregated and bad interracial school experiences can lead a child to acquire discriminating racial attitudes. Many of the essayists indicated that in their childhood, they did not have contact with people of diverse races or ethnicities, nor were they given an adequate history or background information of such groups.

The "I" testimonies further show the importance of teachers in shaping children's views and attitudes. For many of the children, teachers were their heroes and heroines and they looked up to them for guidance. Where teachers were biased and expressed negative attitudes toward children of a different race or ethnicity, children picked up on this and thought it was all right for them to also discriminate against this group. Teachers who encouraged children to interact with their peers, regardless of race, sowed the seeds of tolerance among children and vice versa.

THE WORKPLACE AS A SOCIALIZING AGENT

A significant part of some of our essayists' lives was spent at work. Evidence in the essays shows that the essayists were influenced and affected by racial attitudes they brought or found in the workplace. Traits they developed on the job agreed or negated those valued at home.

In addition to family, school, peer group, and the mass media, the workplace is the dominant institution in most people's lives and, as such, influences people's self-concepts and work roles. By the time all essayists started to work, they had all had *primary socialization*, which is personality development and role learning that occurs during early childhood at home. This early learning in their family settings included the mastery of language, the acquisition of basic skills, and the preparation for experiences outside the family. As we saw above, childhood experiences, including the family, place of residence, social class, and religion, influenced the essayists' personalities and their perceptions of those who were different from the essayists themselves.

From home, school, and college, the essayists learned society's central cultural values, including those pertaining to race and ethnicity. In many cases, school, college, peers, and television managed to change the essayists' attitudes and behavior toward those who were different from them. This happened because the socializing process is complex, involving many agencies that can impart different, and sometimes conflicting, values and norms.

In the workplace, and on the playground, the essayists underwent a process of *resocialization* when they abandoned, or reaffirmed, their home-grown attitudes about people who were different from them. This resocialization began when they left home and went to school, where they played with peers who challenged their family values about race, religion, and ethnicity, either positively or negatively. Eventually, the workplace and/or playground became the stage, where they acted out their family, school, or church scripts.

At the playground, some essayists were astounded to hear their peers and parents shouting out racial slurs, as they excitedly cheered the game. This brought out the views of those parents who might not have been candid or bold enough to utter such slurs in the presence of their own child. So the excitement of the game brought out the bigot in them. At some workplaces, the stereotypes carried from home, and validated or invalidated at school and by television, are exchanged between minorities and majorities in an equal-to-equal mutual exchange of racial sentiments.

In the workplace, majority essayists confronted racism for the first time ever. In some places, the work force was dominated by minorities. This enabled the majority essayists to experience the challenges of being a minority for the first time: the feelings of alienation, and those of being a misfit. This unnerved them. For the first time, also, the majority essayists learned the stereotypes and caricatures that minorities carry of the majority. The workplace facilitated both the majority and the minority to try to clarify the stereotypes that each had about the other. They did this by speaking these stereotypes out loud or by basing their reaction to each other on a stereotype or two, especially in the quest for an appropriate work relationship. Through a test/counter-test method, the workers reached a point of clarification that made them comfortable with each other. This revelation, or rather *resocialization*, improved their work relationships. However, in those work situations where there was no direct discussion of behavior based on mutual stereotypes, no Socratic dialectical discourse occurred to bring the parties to a higher level of racial relations. As a result, the stereotypes ended up as the private interpretations of the behavior of those who are assumed to fit the stereotype.

These workplace stories anchor the point that prejudice cannot be reduced without a meaningful dialogue about differences and similarities between parties. That is why there was turnover in those workplaces where people pointed fingers at each other, based on hidden stereotypes, but did not reach a point of dialogue.

In conclusion, we contend that in the workplace, as people carve out their niches and demarcate their turf, they want to be sure that their fellow workers fit in with the work group. If a worker is of the majority group, minority workers will want to test him or her for racism. They do not want to get stuck for years with a bigot on a job that has its own strains. If he or she is a minority, the majority too would test him or her to see if he or she fits their stereotypes. They want to know if he or she is different from "those people."

When parties trade stereotypes and dramatize them through caricatures and test/counter-test character games, they can laugh together as a catharsis. Revealing that these stereotypes are flawed uplifts everybody from the platonic metaphoric cave of ignorance, where each is mesmerized by shadows, into the light of reality about each other. This usually heals the animosity among fellow workers and elevates each person to a more trusting level, so that they judge each other as individuals, rather than as embodiments of a group. When this happens, the parties are *resocialized* to the innocence of childhood once more, when they played with other children and judged them as individuals, not as members of some group.

TRIBAL AMERICA IN THE MAKING?

This study on race and ethnicity in the United States bares similarities to a study conducted by Beckett and O'Connell (1977) of university students in Nigeria. In their study, the researchers concluded that while ethnicity shaped people's behavior, there were many exceptions. University students considered membership of the same ethnic group a relatively unimportant factor in the selection of their husbands and wives, just like our U.S. essayists showed that higher education liberalized their attitudes toward racial, ethnic, and religious differences.

Through our formal research and long-term observation, we are aware of the revulsion that the great majority of college students feel for the competitive ethnicity that Africans call tribalism and Americans call racism. As shown by our essayists, American students also abhor racism, although many of them are unequivocal on interracial marriage because it brings them and their family blame from either side of the racial or ethnic or religious divide. This is by no means true for all the essayists.

Beckett and O'Connell also found that Nigerian university students retained strong ethnic affiliations in terms of culture and social ties, but they do not want to be personally ethnic. In the same way, American students also maintain strong relations based on skin color but do not want to be thought of as racist. Both the Nigerian and American students want their countries to get rid of ethnic/racial politics. At the same time, the events of the past and present show how political and social crises may force the majority of even the most highly educated stratum of society to retreat, at least temporarily, behind ethnic and racial lines for Nigerians and Americans, respectively. But if, under certain circumstances, most of the students are potential "tribalists" or "racists," we think it is important to emphasize that they are never more than reluctant tribalists or racists.

Both racism in the United States and tribalism in Africa are the predication of policies based on race or tribe for the purpose of subordinating a racial or tribal group and maintaining control over that group. That has been the practice of many countries over the years. Racism, like tribalism, is not necessarily composed of overt discriminatory attitudes and acts by individual dominators over the dominated. Racism, like tribalism, is also subtly embedded in the normal operations of established social institutions such as marriage and family, community, schools, colleges and universities, the workplace, and the playground, as illustrated by our essayists. It is also manifested in religion, economics, entertainment, health, and other sectors of a country. Often an institution's operating rules or policies are spelled out to be fair and unbiased. They may be laid down as laws or expected as mores and folkways, but they are unbiased only on the surface. In practice, they work against those in the discriminated outer group by the clique of the inner group. This was abundantly illustrated by those essayists whose parents or churches taught them to love, while the parents and churches themselves indulged in discriminatory behavior. Such institutionalized racism, we feel, constitutes a state of tribalism, where the minorities in America live in a tribal status—in political, economic, and social dimensions, in a similar way to how the dominant tribes in third-world tribal societies peripheralize the weaker and smaller tribes.

Racism, just like tribalism, can thus be overt or covert. It is overt when it is *de jure*, as in South Africa before F. W. de Klerk lost power to Nelson Mandela. It is covert and *de facto* when there are laws against it, as in the United States. It takes three related forms—at the micro-, macro-, and megalevels. At the microlevel, individual members of one ethnic or racial group might fight against another group, or the total population of one racial or ethnic group might gang up against the total population of another ethnic or racial group. We call the first individual racism, like the one our essayists described. It consists of overt acts by individuals that cause death, injury, or the violent destruction of property. Macrolevel racism and megalevel racism are at the national and international levels, respectively. At the second and third levels, racism is far more subtle, less identifiable in terms of specific individuals committing the acts. Institutional racism originates in the operation of established and respected forces in society. It is based on the way things have always been, with the rewards and threats going to those who have always received them. This may be based on skin color or it may be tribal in the sense of the benefits going to the tribe that prospered from the investment and the rewards of the colonial government.

Tribalism is one of the most disruptive influences confronting African states. It is the basis for hatred between peoples within the same country as well as between countries. It leads to nepotism, corruption, and other evils, such as civil wars and military coups that have devastated educational and other social-political institutions. Like racism, tribalism is on the rise in the United States. We see this especially in times of crisis, as when some groups, such as the militia and other disgruntled elements, resort to bombing public places, such as the Oklahoma Federal Building, or when riots erupt following a legal verdict, deemed to be unfair to the "tribes," such as the one that followed the Rodney King verdict in Los Angeles.

When this state of anomie occurs in Africa, the leaders usually turn to their group for tribal support and loyalty. In the United States, nativists cry out to their government or even run for congressional seats, so that they can legislate against the rights of other tribes that they perceive as threats to their tribal supremacy. Other tribes resort to violence to change laws that they consider to be unfair and unjust.

The tribe in the American sense then is a group of people with similar deeply held convictions about the need to advance the welfare of their group members even if this happens at the expense of everyone else. For the tribe, the end justifies the means. Loyalty to the tribe in Africa has created untold hardships and greatly wounded the national psyche in many countries. The same catastrophe could befall the United States, or any other developed country, if tribal interests are not subsumed for the greater good of the nation-state.

Africa failed to acknowledge its multitribal character and to develop a multicultural policy that will accommodate the needs of the various groups within its borders. After independence, most national leaders turned the national governments into tribal governments that promoted the interests of a few tribes and ignored the concerns of the weaker and smaller tribes. Our fear is that the strife that engulfs Africa today might befall the United States if the majority tribe refuses to accept diversity and to give the smaller and weaker tribes the opportunities to participate on an equal footing in the development of the country and in sharing the benefits that result therefrom. This is evidenced by current efforts to renege on the Emancipation Proclamation and to reverse the gains of the Civil Rights Act of 1964.

PUBLIC POLICY AND RACE RELATIONS

A litany of American racial, ethnic, and religious woes could fill this page, especially if we probed its history. Fortunately, so could a list of the country's efforts to effectively deal with these troubles. But taking the step from merely stating the ills to successfully handling them has been—and will continue to be—extremely difficult. For now, and as we enter the next century, the question remains a simple one: Can America be saved from racial and ethnic tension?

Reducing social distance and prejudice will likely gain prominence in the public arena as we enter the twenty-first century. This is because the survival of American democracy will depend on the extent to which there is mutual coexistence between the diverse groups that will increasingly inhabit the country. So far, public policy has made great strides in reducing discrimination but little has been done to lessen prejudice. This may be because the factors that lead to prejudice are beyond public policy. As this study has shown, family up-bringing plays a significant role in the formation of perceptions and prejudices about different races and ethnic groups. Yet, government cannot legislate how parents should raise their children. Even so, reducing prejudice is essential since it is the root cause of discrimination.

Although this study has unveiled new evidence of the troubles facing America, many Americans will likely greet this newest presentation of America's ills with a collective yawn: base language, racism, prejudice, intolerance, America is in danger. So what's new? Plenty. The immense task ahead has become even more staggering because of the increasing diversity of America's population. The most helpless victims, as we learned from the essayists, are the children, both minority and majority, whose parents are imposing racial biases upon their *tabula rasa*, innocent minds. Parents tell their children not to be prejudiced while they themselves practice prejudice. Pious churches preach a theocracy that all are one, while every Sunday most churches remain racially segregated and fight to keep it that way. Parents teach tolerance but move out of neighborhoods that are becoming mixed. Children are told not to use racial slurs, but parents are the first to use them in the heat of excitement. Schools teach diversity, but teachers remain aloof to racial tensions on school campuses. The workplace is becoming diverse, but fellow workers hardly communicate to each other about the stereotypes that keep them apart.

Parents and societal change institutions seem oblivious to the reality of America. Typical America contains many racial and ethnic groups. Nearly 22 million (9%) report themselves as being of Hispanic origin, and over 7 million (2.9%) identify themselves as Asian-Pacific Islanders. African Americans number 30 million, or 12% of the population, and the Native American/Eskimo/Aleut populations make up about 2 million (0.8%). That leaves over 177 million (71.3%) people who consider themselves to be White-non-Hispanic. Just over 21 million of us were not born in America, but call it home. Every year, almost 25% of America's population growth comes from immigration. America speaks many languages: over 31 million Americans speak a language other than English at home; over half of them speak Spanish (*The World Almanac and Book of Facts 1997*). Children should not be robbed by their parents, their churches, and their schools of the opportunity to experience this diversity and to learn how to work within it.

As schools, neighborhoods, and workplaces are becoming more mixed now than before, this reduction in segregation may be associated with a decrease in prejudice, but the two are different. Our findings indicate that prejudice is far more resistant to public policy and poses a far greater threat to the ungluing of the fabric of this country than does discrimination. This is because discrimination is the outward manifestation of prejudice, which is often invisible.

The problem, as we see it and as testified by the essayists, is arch conservatism. This is an ideology that is predicated on maintaining the *status quo* and that is antiforeign and reclusive in its outlook. As we saw in the essays, conservative parents resort to hidden violence against other groups, in their language and attitude, and seek to recruit their own children as members of their conservative group. In America today, the extreme Right uses base language, superiority complex, fear, racism, antigovernment propaganda, and appeal to emotions to bash those who belong to a different ethnicity, race, or religion. In a few instances, such as the bombing of the Oklahoma Federal Building, such people have reacted to diversity in America by resorting to violence to achieve their goal of isolationism. America must refrain from the slippery slope of arch conservatism so that its policies, especially those pertaining to diversity, are not shaped by a tendency to ignore reality, but rather acknowledge and face the challenge of diversity. How this should be done is the subject of the concluding section.

SOME MODEST PROPOSALS

In this section, we outline several suggestions for addressing the problems of prejudice and racism. The proposals address the problems we identified with family upbringing of children, the work environment, and the influence of schools and peers.

Family and Community

One of the thorniest issues in ameliorating race relations is the seeming impotence of public policy in addressing the family's influence in instilling prejudice in children. We suggest three ways for addressing this problem. First, we propose that model multicultural neighborhoods should be promoted by the Department of Housing and Urban Development. Second, we suggest a more vigorous effort by communities to increase neighborhood integration, and third, we advocate parental education. These proposals are fleshed out below.

First, since a continued and sustained interaction between the races has been found to reduce prejudice among children, we suggest that the Department of Housing and Urban Development promulgate policies and programs for model neighborhoods to demonstrate how diverse racial and ethnic groups can amicably live together. We suggest there be such model neighborhoods in every state. The model neighborhoods should reproduce the old extended family structure on a new basis of affinity that is built around the present-day dictates of a multicultural world.

The multicultural-affinity family neighborhood will be made up of several families numbering anywhere from ten to one hundred people inhabiting several blocks within a city. These blocks together then form neighborhoods of approximately three thousand people of which several, linked together, and diverse in race and ethnicity, make up the multicultural community. A new relationship between different ethnic and racial groups will result from proximity on a scale unprecedented in human history and offer people a chance to develop richer relationships, to increase and to deepen communication, and to heighten the capacity for creative experience. Eventually, as these model neighborhoods grow across the country, they will provide the social laboratories in which improvement can be made for subsequent replication throughout the nation.

We believe that only in multicultural-affinity family neighborhoods will children be given a chance to cultivate their own ideas and interests away from continuous adult supervision of whom they play with. Family, church, and school in these neighborhoods will facilitate the freewill interaction of children with each other. Parents who seek to suppress their children's personal dissension for the avowed purpose of preserving their race, ethnic group, or religion are in fact swindling their children because when personal initiative and individual freedom are lost, crowdism, conformism, and mass or mob attitudes emerge, which eventually block social progress. Such parental remedies are more dangerous to children's development of healthy interracial attitudes than the wrongs they pretend to cure.

The essays in this book show that young people are all the more vulnerable to hurt when they are sheltered from the reality of ethnic, religious, and racial diversity in America. Today, the family as an institution is at the threshold of a new revolution occasioned by the information age, high international migration, and the service-industrial revolution, all of which are threatening the consanguineous family, perhaps as never before. This globalization has caused a new wave of immigration of people from the third-world to the industrialized world, just as it has led to the introduction of Western and Japanese capital in the third-world for cheap labor and raw materials. Third-world immigration is making such countries as the United States even more multiracial and multiethnic, just as multinational corporations are changing the socioscapes of the third-world.

In this interdependent world, our essayists show us that some parents still hold an archaic image of the family, and want to pass on that image to their children. Some parents still have that nostalgic, romantic view of the family as being composed of grandparents, parents, and children, who once formed a community in its own right, usually composed of people of the same race or tribe.

Today the wholesome family closeness that is based on race is no longer tenable. Yet, the idea of deliberately producing multicultural-affinity families to strengthen the community is not yet accepted practice. We believe that much of the training for life that young people will require for the next century and in the unfolding new world will be based on how well they master skills for multicultural social relationships, and the appreciation of diversity. Therefore, we need to master the art of creating a multiracial-multiethnic-affinity family structure that gives the young living examples and experiences of social cohesion that will enable them to live in a changing multicultural society. This can start with the promotion of model multicultural neighborhoods.

Second, a disturbing trend in the demographics of the United States is the increase in the residential and geographic disparities of racial and ethnic groups. According to an analysis by Frey, "the distribution of U.S. Whites across geographic regions and metro areas is becoming increasingly dissimilar to that of faster growing minorities" (Frey 1991, 6). This trend forebodes problems for intercultural understanding. For, as our essayists made abundantly clear, lack of interaction between the races leads to intolerance and prejudice. To forestall such a problem, efforts must be made to reduce residential and geographic isolation of the different races and ethnic groups. One way to approach this problem is to require municipalities to establish benchmarks for reducing racial segregation. This can be measured using the segregation index. This goal should be part of the Annual Housing Plans of municipalities. Such a requirement would make Community Development Block Grant (CDBG) funding conditional on meeting such targets.

In addition, programs to increase the mix of housing types in single-family neighborhoods and in suburbs will also give low-income and minority households the opportunity to live in these neighborhoods and could help reduce residential segregation. This requires a change in zoning laws to allow for mixed residential housing types. Support for traditional neighborhood design ordinances could help achieve this goal. Even so, such a program must be complemented with vigilance over "blockbusting" techniques by real estate agents and "redlining" by banks that deny minority households the choice of residence and equal access to mortgage loans.

A number of cities now have Human Relations Councils with the objective of promoting intercultural understanding between the races. Human Relations

Councils are statutory organizations established by local governments to examine the racial problems of communities and to craft ways for improving racial tolerance. In one Midwestern city, an award is presented each year to a person in the community who demonstrates excellence in promoting racial understanding. Such a program can be emulated by cities that are looking for ways to address the racial and ethnic problems of their communities. Since each community is unique, the task of the council would vary. If the problem identified in a community is religious intolerance, then the Human Relations Council would target efforts in this area. If, on the other hand, the problem is one of discrimination toward recent immigrants, then educational efforts by the council could be implemented to educate the community about the immigrant group.

Third, as the testimonies by the students have shown, a lot of parents are in denial about their prejudices, although these are made evident unconsciously to their children. Therefore, parents must be brought to a greater awareness of their values and biases and must seek help. Multicultural parenting lessons should be required as part of the parenting classes that are given to new and expectant parents at hospitals and family-planning clinics. Such lessons should be required for the accreditation of hospitals and clinics by the state and federal governments. Topics to be covered in such parenting classes should include "raising the nonracist child," and "living in a multicultural society."

Education

The proposals we make for addressing problems in the educational system are meant to (1) reduce acts by minorities that help to perpetuate prejudice against them, and (2) enhance intercultural interaction. These proposals pertain to both formal and informal education. The first set of proposals is geared at helping minorities cope with years of discrimination and at helping them develop self-esteem. To accomplish this task, we suggest that eupraxophy centers (community-based learning centers which offer educational opportunities for the public with the objective of instilling the values of love, self-esteem, and peaceful coexistence, as well as entrepreneurship and functional literacy courses) be established in minority communities to teach self-love and self-esteem lessons to members of minority groups. After years under the yoke of bigotry and discrimination, members of minority groups develop inferiority complexes and act out in ways that are often damaging to themselves and further perpetuate the perceptions that people have of this group. Therefore, self-esteem lessons should be offered to minority groups to help them unlearn these harmful reactionary traits.

Eupraxophy centers can be run by the Urban League or by the statutory Human Relations Councils. The centers can be located in offices of local Community Development Corporations or in churches. For the most alienated "hard-core" youth in the inner city, the education programs could be held by storefronts or on streets. In these eupraxophy centers, self-love and self-esteem lessons should not only be taught to minorities, but also to members of the majority group, who might not have had a chance to intellectually interact with minorities. The majority group could team up on neutral ground to discuss its similarities and differences with minority groups.

We suggest self-love and self-esteem lessons because in the 1960s Malcom X, Martin Luther King, Jr., Eldridge Cleaver, and other sagacious African American intellectuals spoke about the self-hatred that Black people have for themselves and each other. The works of Amiri Baraka and James Baldwin are filled with characters masking their anger and rage and turning it back on themselves as self-hatred. This self-hate, developed from European disinformation campaigns that defamed the non-European cultures and exalted Western civilization as "universal" and good for all. As a result, epithets such as "primitive," "superstitious," and "lower-level on the evolutionary ladder" were used to characterize the non-European.

Minority youth and adults need lessons about how to overcome this aspect of self-hatred consciousness, the painful self-negation and self-scrutiny that obsesses oppressed people. Such an attitude must be eliminated before minorities can work meaningfully for themselves and with those who are different from them.

In America, both Whites and Blacks developed a Tarzan-like image of Africa. Langston Hughes wrote that his patron, Mrs. Mason, wanted him to be primitive and know and feel the intuitions of the primitive (Berry 1983). To some extent, the reduction of prejudice, especially against Africans and African Americans in America, shall come from the African continent, delivering itself from the image of Tarzan, so that its peoples on the continent and those in the diaspora do not carry the stigma of the twentieth century into the next. The continued exploitation and ensuing underdevelopment of the African continent by developed nations in collaboration with corrupt indigenous "independent" regimes on the continent gives support to those who view the Black race as befitting of second-class citizenship in the family of nations. As a result, reducing prejudice against Blacks in the United States will require that significant social and econo-political progress be made by African countries to reduce civil strife, poverty, and economic decline.

In order to do this, Africans and African Americans must seek each other out in an economic intercourse for mutual benefit. This business intercourse will bolster both peoples and exalt their status in the community of humans. We are aware that Euro-American and Japanese business is already well established on the African continent. If African Americans, Africans, or any other minorities are going to have pride in themselves in a world where capitalism has been globalized, they need to invest and own successful companies, not only in the United States, but around the world. Eupraxophy centers could help enlighten minorities, African Americans in particular, about business opportunities, entrepreneurship, and management skills. Eupraxophy Centers will be where dangers of degradation shall be brought to the forefront of consciences, subsequently becoming synchronized into *eupraxophy* (*eupraxis* - good action; *sophia* - scientific and philosophical wisdom)—a set of convictions and practices (technologies) offering a cosmic outlook and an ethical guide to the good life independent of natural determinism (Maslow 1969).

In the eupraxophy centers, students would be actively recruited by street workers and taught by volunteers and other staff members who generally reside in the local community. Eupraxophy centers can be outstandingly successful because (1) the curriculum is chosen to be of interest to the student rather than to satisfy the assumed requirements of a far-off board of education, and (2) students are likely to identify well with staff who are personally familiar with their backgrounds and behavior patterns. Many of the disadvantaged youth who graduate from the storefront schools could go on to enroll in "academies," where the specific purpose is to give additional preparation for college.

Second, in order to increase integration and improve intercultural understanding, we propose that a domestic student exchange (DSE) program, similar to that organized by the American Field Service, be implemented in schools in collaboration with social service workers. The DSE program would encourage students to spend time away from their parent school and to live and experience a culture that is different from their own. It would allow students to spend a semester or two in host schools. By so doing, students will not only get to interact with those of a different race or ethnic group, but it will also offer them an opportunity to form long-lasting friendships with children of other cultures.

A White middle-class student, for example, might spend a semester at a predominantly Jewish school and learn about the Jewish religion and culture. An inner-city African American child could spend several weeks with a suburban White family, and a student from a White family in a rural area or suburb could spend time studying and living in the inner city. This exposure would enable the children to see a different perspective of America than what they are used to, and could go a long way in addressing the cultural alienation that many of the essayists lamented about in their life stories. The responsibility falls on states to encourage these programs by making funds available for their implementation.

At the college level, the focus should be on increasing diversity at the universities. That means increasing the number of minority students in predominantly White institutions and also increasing the number of White students in predominantly Black institutions. Realistically, however, the problem is more that of attracting minorities to White colleges than the other way around. Colleges must endeavor to create programs that facilitate open discussion and interaction between students of diverse racial and ethnic backgrounds.

Predominantly White liberal arts colleges were not designed or established with the cultural, academic, or social adjustment needs of minority students in mind. These needs must be recognized and addressed programmatically if we expect minority students to successfully challenge and overcome the frustrations of culture shock and isolation in these institutions. A true commitment to campus diversity should include support for minority cultures. A most frustrating experience for minorities, especially African American students, is when White professors and administrators do not recognize African American culture, history, and cultural activities as legitimate. Outside of generally limited African American history course offerings, the many contributions made by Black people in other disciplines are usually nonexistent in college curricula.

It is sometimes misunderstood when minority students or educational researchers contend that there is hostility toward minority people on predominantly White campuses. Such issues as discrimination by campus security or the presence of racist signs or slogans are understood better than the more subtle hostility that is often present in curriculum content or instructional methodology.

For example, course content that demeans minorities or denies their existence is hostile. Bibliographies that cite no African American researchers or writers are hostile. Instructors who do not allow African American students to write on African American issues or who downgrade them for doing so are engaging in hostile acts.

Justice to minority students and correcting the distortions of White students' realities will require a thorough examination of curriculum and instruction, as well as curricular and instructional modifications. Faculty are likely to require some in-service training and to need consultant assistance for revising curriculum. Among the national organizations that could provide trainer and consultant assistance are the National Alliance for Black School Educators (NABSE), the National Council for Black Studies (NCBS), and the African Heritage Studies Association (AHSA).

An Office of Minority Affairs should be used to proactively articulate these and other issues with faculty, administrators, and students on predominantly White liberal arts campuses. Regularly scheduled workshops, lectures, and cultural programs designed to enlighten and educate at all levels can help create an atmosphere for open cultural exchange and communication. But most important, such programming helps minority students to stay in touch with their heritage and identities.

At a macrolevel, we suggest that a national minority affairs conference should be held every academic year to focus on the elements of institutional environments that form a positive learning community for all races. This conference should convene specifically to find resolutions to the ongoing problems of recruiting and retaining minority students, faculty, and staff at predominantly White colleges. College staff should envision developing a model by which colleges across the country, with similar problems, could be utilized as a resource to maintain ethnically and culturally diverse academic communities. Task-oriented workshops, designed to maximize participant involvement, should provide realistic recommendations to be further cultivated and researched by each college so that each college administrator has an empathetic feel of the problems in his or her midst, instead of the xenophobic apathy that this study reveals.

We recognize that many Board of Trustees have made a commitment to campus diversity. What is lacking is a follow through on these policies. There is a lack of monitoring of the policy to see how well universities are meeting their goal of diversifying college campuses. We recommend that a subcommittee of the board should conduct a yearly evaluation of the policy's implementation and report to the full board. It should be the board's responsibility to rearticulate its policy on campus diversity at least once a year, if not more frequently.

It is also essential that colleges create a positive environment in which students and faculty of diverse cultures feel comfortable. Specific efforts should be undertaken to build elements into the college environment that will assist African American and other minority students to develop or enhance their self-esteem. Such elements would include, for example, minority family and administrator models, curriculum that depicts, truthfully, the historical and contemporary contributions of people of minority descent, as well as guest lecturers, campus entertainment, cultural activities that are representative of minority culture, and the inclusion in campus media of minority interests and concerns. The creation of a positive campus environment will require the cooperation of all important components of campus life.

Administration, faculty, student government, minority student organizations, fraternities and sororities, athletic teams, campus media, and alumni should all be brought into dialogue to reach consensus on goals and to develop a plan of implementation. Respect for, and the inclusion of, minority culture into the total campus fabric can result in benefits to all students and thus, to the total college community. Minority students are likely to be reinforced in the pride of their heritage and a belief of their own personal worth. Relieved of the stresses of racial and cultural hostility, these students will be more able to attend to the rigors of academic demands.

White students are also likely to benefit significantly through a reordering of their reality, through coming to grips with the truth about the contribution that various cultures have made to world development. When minority and White students interact in an environment that is based on historical reality, with mutual respect and dignity, the entire campus community is well served.

The presence of minority faculty, staff, and administrators on campus is important for minority student retention. Minority faculty and administrators are models of achievement and are potential mentors and resources to assist students with adjustment to campus life. In addition to the cultural and psychological benefits minority professionals may bring to minority students, minority faculty and administrators also provide a support system for each other. Just as minority students often feel isolated and alienated in a predominantly White environment, so do minority professionals. Thus, minority professionals are in need of their fellow professionals to provide friendship and cultural support. Where there are only one or two minority professionals on campus, they, too, are likely to become "dropouts," especially if they are unmarried.

The recruitment of minority faculty and administrators will involve more than national searches. Recruitment may have to involve various creative efforts, such as consortia of colleges establishing doctoral support programs to train and develop minority faculty. Temporary measures might also involve such programs as visiting scholars-in-residence or a series of guest lecturers.

Colleges should make additional financial commitments to minority faculty and staff to attract and retain qualified personnel. Some specific possibilities include: (1) differential salaries, better fringe benefits, and incentives for this restricted market; (2) release time to do the additional counseling, advising, and mentoring required by minority students; (3) more frequent sabbaticals, particularly for those working on isolated campuses; and (4) opportunities for educational exchanges and consultation among minority and White faculty. Responsibility for this exchange should reside with the chief academic officer.

Finally, minority students, faculty, and staff coming to isolated areas must function within two distinct environments—the college community and the wider community (i.e., city or town) in which the college is located. It is important for the wider community to be sensitized to the cultural needs of the new minority members who have now become a part of the environment's cultural structure. In such cases, the college should take a leadership role in educating the wider community (i.e., elementary and high schools, churches, police, etc.) about the cultural and social needs of the minority community. Communities that are not aware of the cultural needs of minority groups matriculating within their environments could adversely affect the ability of these people to survive and successfully become a part of the community.

The Workplace

The essayists have testified to the importance of a cordial work environment in the promotion of better race relations. Increasingly, many corporations have come to the realization that attention to workplace diversity makes good business sense. Workplaces are currently at different stages of diversity acceptance: most are in the awareness stage, some still deny the problems and the opportunities that come with valuing a diverse work force, but a few pioneers are formulating and implementing long-range plans and educating the work force. In order to improve workplace interaction among people of diverse ethnic and cultural backgrounds, we suggest the following:

First, workplaces must acknowledge that diversity is a reality. Census demographics indicate that White women and minorities will account for a majority of the net growth in the nation's labor force. Therefore, respecting and cultivating an environment that supports a diverse work force is a bottom-line issue. This should therefore be incorporated into the mission, vision, and strategic plans of companies. Diversity initiatives must be tied to the business plan and be a vital part of the long-range change process. Isolated training sessions, speakers, and ethnic cuisine celebrations do not make a highly functioning racially and or ethnically diverse work force. Workers who are made aware that their company is serious about maintaining and promoting a diverse work force are also likely to change their attitudes toward people who are different from them.

Second, workplaces (businesses, government departments, nongovernmental organizations) should evaluate the outcomes of their plans regularly. Plans should be evaluated on the basis of what actually happens and not on good intentions. The best strategic plans are outcome based rather than problem centered. Therefore, it pays for workplaces to be proactive about their vision for diversity rather than reactive, after anger, conflict, turnovers, boycotts, and lawsuits have occurred. In line with this, it is important that companies celebrate small successes in the accomplishment of their diversity targets. This should be done at least once a year. Third, workplace interaction must also be actively promoted between workers of diverse races and ethnicities. The more informal the interaction, the better. To accomplish this task, we suggest that *Cafe au Lait* work breaks be set aside at the workplace when workers can meet and interact with their fellow workers and trade stories about their upbringing and prejudices. This we have found, in the stories shared by the essayists, to be beneficial to workers and helps to unlearn some of the prejudices that people bring along to work. Invited speakers could also be brought in by management to guide semiformal discussions during this time. In order to provide incentive for businesses to implement these programs, firms should be given tax breaks by the federal government.

CONCLUSION

In our view, race relations in the United States remain strained despite democratic and civil rights legislation. Apartheid, American style, on the wane since the 1960s, is taking a long time to disappear totally. This study reveals that we have not yet reaped harmony in a world of great difference, but we must not settle for less. We postulate that in the twenty-first century, domestic issues will assume ascendancy and threaten national security far more than external threats. Of these, race relations and how to manage cultural and ethnic diversity will be paramount on the domestic front. Therefore, race relations will have to be treated with the same sense of urgency that the country dealt with national security during the cold war. Thus, America will have to look at the "enemy within" not "the enemy without" in drafting its future national security policy.

Bibliography

Banks, James A. *Teaching Strategies for Ethnic Studies.* 5th ed. Boston: Allyn and Bacon, 1991.

Beckett, Paul, and James O'Connell. *Education and Power in Nigeria.* New York: Africa Printing Publishing Company, 1977.

Berry, Faith. *Langston Hughes: Before and Beyond Harlem.* Westport, Connecticut: Lawrence Hill and Company, 1983.

Du Bois, W. E. B. *The Souls of Black Folk.* New York: Dover Publications, Inc., 1994.

Frey, William H. "Are Two Americas Emerging?" *Population Today*, October 1991, 6-8.

Maslow, Abraham H. "*Eupsychia*—The Good Society." *Journal of Humanistic Psychology*, Vol. 1, No. 2, Fall 1961, 1-8.

Morris, Jeanne. "Indirect Influences on Children's Racial Attitudes." *Educational Leadership*, January 1981, 286-288.

Patterson, James, and Peter Kim. *The Day America Told the Truth: What People Really Believe about Everything that Really Matters.* New York: Prentice-Hall , 1991.

Schaefer, Richard T. *Racial and Ethnic Groups.* 4th ed. Scranton, Penn: HarperCollins, 1990.

The World Almanac and Book of Facts 1997. New York: Press Publication Company, 1997.

Index

About the Authors

ALFRED T. KISUBI is Associate Professor at the College of Education and Human Services at the University of Wisconsin-Oshkosh.

MICHAEL A. BURAYIDI is Assistant Professor and Coordinator of the Urban and Regional Studies Program in the Department of Public Affairs at the University of Wisconsin-Oshkosh.